Friendship

MYRON BRENTON

Friendship

STEIN AND DAY / Publishers / New York

First published in 1974
Copyright © 1974 by Myron Brenton
Library of Congress Catalog Card No. 74-78533
All rights reserved
Designed by Ed Kaplin
Printed in the United States of America
Stein and Day/*Publishers*/Scarborough House,
Briarcliff Manor, N.Y. 10510
ISBN 0-8128-1727-3

For
JACK ZANGER
and
GEORGE RIEMER

ACKNOWLEDGMENTS

To write a book on friendship in America is to engage in a process of friendly interaction with scores of people via face-to-face encounters and written communications—to engender exchanges with strangers and near-strangers, with acquaintances and friends. To write such a book is to plumb the feelings of people known and unknown—to pick brains, as the inelegant phrase goes, of lay people and experts in the social sciences.

The viewpoints this work presents are mine, obviously, but in a significant sense the work is a collaboration between myself and all those important others. Almost without exception they gave generously of their thoughts, their emotions, and their observations—in short, of themselves. Many did so under the promise of anonymity. Even those who did not represent a sizable group. How can I list them all? Thank them all?

I can't, of course—but I want them to know how very, very grateful I am.

M.B.

CONTENTS

CONNECTIONS

1

Our Friends, Ourselves

THE moment is pure anguish: the white son is dead; the black son, his slayer, is about to be executed. The two grieving fathers are together, for the white man, having worked through his own anguish, has come to be with the black man. And the black man, at first caged in by grief and bitterness, eventually reaches out in turn. The clock is seconds away from striking four, the hour of the execution. Somehow, out of the mire of hate, desperation, and calamity, a beautiful thing is happening to these two human beings.

The black father, whose beloved son is about to die, says, "I have a friend."

The white father, whose beloved son is already dead, responds, "I have a friend."

So ends *Lost in the Stars,* the classic musical tragedy set in South Africa. It is a moving play throughout, but no moment is as moving, as touching, as thoroughly and nobly human as the one encompassing those last words. Few of us, upon hearing them, fail to be shaken; they have the power to touch deeply.

The words reach us, of course, because we have been privy to the suffering of the two men left alone upon the stage; it is hard not to empathize. But their effect, I think, rests upon more than just a story line. We are reached where it counts. To say, "I have a friend"—to believe, "I have a friend"—is to say and to believe, "I am not alone. There's another who sees me, values me, trusts me, is strengthened by me—another whom I see and value and trust and am strengthened by. We share laughter, we share sorrow; in some measure we share life—no, because I have a friend, and am my friend's friend, neither of us is alone."

Friendship. *Friendship.* A couple of years prior to the writing of this book, when I was forty-three, it somehow came to me, not in a flash but as the culmination of accumulated experiences that seems like a flash, how much my friends mean to me. How, in a very real psychic sense, these friends to whom I am closest enrich me with their affection, reward me with the importance they attach to me, and have enough faith in me to allow me to try to enrich and reward them likewise, to the extent of my capacity. I hadn't thought of my friends in such emotional terms before, at least not in these past several decades that can be said to constitute my adulthood. I was moved, truly so; and as my friendship reverie continued I suddenly seemed to myself larger than life. Larger, certainly, than I had seemed to myself before beginning my musings. These people sought me out. These people respect my judgment (at least enough to ask for, if not always follow, it). These people extend trust and loyalty and affection and concern. Though not tied to me by licenses or laws they moved to share (in part) their lives with me.

In some few cases the sharing between us was more convoluted. It was a sharing of families, theirs and mine, a meshing of selves, mates, and assorted children. And what in time emerged from this periodic clustering of people who had become important to each other was kinship of a different nature—not blood- or marriage-related, but related only by the warm mutual wish to have us be kin.

Inevitably, then, I thought in wider terms: how, out of the complexity of our need for contact we reach out to embrace others, dear ones at home, dear ones outside the home. How we reach out to embrace some this way, some that way, in a configuration of relationships that (hopefully) makes sense in terms of the rank order of our needs. And how these relationships, each an emotional picture puzzle all its own, must harmonize with the others—lest it produce conflict, competition, or disintegration.

Well, at this point the glimmer of insight and good feeling vanished as, for one reason or another, more mundane reality intruded. But at this point, too, the writer part of me began to function, posing questions, wanting to get on with the hunt for answers—questions having to do with our friends and with ourselves, answers that would tell us something about them and about ourselves.

So this exploration of friendship—and, more particularly, friendship in America—came to be launched. It got off the ground with voluminous readings of journal papers and books (there is an astonishing paucity of material specifically related to friendship in much of the social sciences, especially psychology). Then came talks with experts in various relevant disciplines and—most exciting and rewarding of all—extensive interviews with over five hundred Americans of all ages and economic groups across the diverse vastness that marks our country.

One evening found me conducting a seminar on friendship at a meeting of the New York City chapter of Parents Without Partners. A sunny weekend was spent at a retirement community in Maryland. There was the rainy morning I talked to students at a junior high school close to the roar of the Los Angeles International Airport. There were drinks and talks with ex-servicemen at American Legion and Veterans of Foreign Wars posts in Massachusetts, North Carolina, Ohio, and elsewhere. There were interviews with suburbanites around Minneapolis and with teenagers at the Midwood Adolescent Project, a rap center in Brooklyn, N.Y. A virtual cornucopia of information came from groups of children on the one hand and adults on the other, who filled out extensive questionnaires on friendship. And so it went, on and on, as I conducted this exploration into American friendships.

It is often said of writers of fiction that as they get into their stories the characters come alive, move and act as if blood really flowed through them, as if they had overcome the handicap of

13

being merely figments of the writers' imaginations. In a different sense the same thing can happen to a writer who deals with facts. Those facts take on a peculiar and particular life, cleave unto themselves to form fascinating and unexpected truths—or, at least, truths as seen through the prism of the writer's eye. Truth or bias, early into the interviews, several things became evident to me and they have strongly influenced the book's approach.

First: when we talk about our friends—more to the point, when we think carefully about them and about our relationships with them—a little magic occurs. We are forced to think more carefully about ourselves. We learn something new about ourselves. This occurred a number of times during the interviews—with a girl at the University of Wisconsin, with a man just checking into that retirement community in Maryland, with a worker on the cavernous floor of an electrical plant in Winston-Salem, North Carolina —with others almost everywhere I sought to inform myself about people's friendships.

When the magic took place it would trigger a signal of some sort from the person I was interviewing. A sign—perhaps a sigh, a glint in the eye, a wondering smile—would mark the end of the interview, followed by a remark along the lines of, "You know, I never really thought about these things before—I'm going to have to do some more thinking." Exchanges via questionnaires were more impersonal, of course, but even so the spell occasionally happened, for now and then a note would accompany the completed form: "This came at the right time for me." It was usually sent by someone young, obviously by someone in the process of attempting to arrive at a better understanding of himself or herself. So: this book is about friendship. This book is about ourselves.

Second: as I researched the ways of friendship of the ancients, of primitive tribes, and of contemporary Americans, I kept being reminded again and again how really universal the experience of friendship is. Everywhere and in all ages people have formed this very same tie with each other—this tie that is not based on the binding forces of kinship, marriage, or romance.

In many ways, of course, approaches to friendship have differed radically among dissimilar groups of people in differing situations or societies. Even among ourselves in the United States we differ somewhat in the way we pattern our friendships: the adolescent unlike the oldster, the factory worker unlike the executive, the city dweller unlike the suburbanite, the young single unlike the middle-aged married person, men unlike women.

As much as we differ, however, we share a common humanity and therefore common designs in our friendships. This became so clear when I looked at anthropological studies of tribes and groups completely unlike us and then compared them with us. For instance: the Didinga of West Africa have an enforced "best friend" system; the Tangu of New Guinea require friends to tell each other of their illicit sexual adventures on pain of death; the Bhumji of India, a Hindu tribe, structures special companionate friendships between wives of different castes who have the same number of children. What do we have in common with the Didinga, the Tangu, and the Bhumji? A reaching out, a need to make contact with other people. A using of the friendship to achieve certain tangible goals. A recognition (explicit or implicit) that friendship no less than other first-rank relationships requires something of us as well as promising something for us in return.

How universal our feelings about friendship are is something that became so very apparent whenever I compared the writings of philosophers and essayists of old with the words of American men and women of the present. Thus, around 50 B.C., the Roman orator Cicero wrote, "It appears then that genuine friendship cannot possibly exist where one of the parties is unwilling to hear truth and the other is equally indisposed to speak it"; it was a twenty-seven-year-old legal secretary in Washington , D.C., who said of her close friends, "I'm able to be truthful, be myself, knowing love and respect will be maintained and grow." Thus close to the sixteenth century the French author Montaigne said of a friend, "If a man should opportune me to give a reason why I loved him, I find it could no otherwise be expressed than by making answer: because it was he, because it was I"; as we near the end of the twentieth century, a Denver lady in her sixties, referring to her oldest friend, said, "We have a feeling for each other. . . . She's she and I'm me and there has been a spark between us that's never extinguished itself."

It is easy to find people who will, basing their ideas on

immediate impressions, talk about regional differences in terms of friendliness. Minnesotans, for instance, supposedly stretch out their arms in brotherly and sisterly affection (though I discovered plenty of Minnesotans who complained about unfriendly neighbors); New Yorkers are supposedly cold and unfriendly (though it is in no way difficult to find New Yorkers involved in deep friendships). And so on. Yet the feeling of universality hit hard again when I talked to Americans who had lived enough and traveled enough to see beyond the apparent regional differences—who recognized that friendliness and friendship are not necessarily synonymous. "I have lived all over the country and basically saw no difference in the way people conducted their friendship," wrote a retired army officer. "Great differences on the surface, great similarities underneath," is the way a Denver businesswoman put it. And a divorcee in New Jersey, who has lived up and down the Eastern seaboard, noted, "Fundamentally, people are all made of the same stuff. They're human. They may work out their lives and problems differently, but at one time or another all feel the need to communicate with someone else."

Third: very early into the work of the book I saw that some intelligent and concerned people were going to expect me to make sweeping judgments about our friendships. At least they had no hesitancy in making them. Friendship in America? My dear, you know how shallow Americans are in their relationships; they don't know the meaning of the word. Friendship in America? Go to France or Italy or Iran or Japan—those people can teach us a thing or two about friendship. Friendship in America? Thirty years ago —fifty years ago—that's when people really knew how to form deep friendships, that's when they really cared about each other; it's too late now.

But as I listened to them, faintly envious at first of the sureness with which they talked about "my" subject, I soon realized that I could not write the book they expected. I was failing to come up with easy, invidious comparisons.

American life is not a smoothly flowing river, especially now and particularly in the more intimate relationships between people. There are too many societal swirls and eddies presently; too many paradoxes, contradictions, exceptions; too many distinctions in terms of where people are situated in their life cycles.

Beyond the exceptions is the basic fact that generalizations with respect to any aspect of functioning—friendship included—cannot take into account the complexities of human interaction. Urbanites may be a "faceless people" by small-town standards, but that truth totally ignores the truth of how they build their own unique communities. Friendships in certain foreign countries may be longer-lasting and more intense than ours—but to let it go at that is to ignore the cost, a cost many of us would not be willing to pay. Mobility makes for transitory relationships, but it does not inevitably follow that they must be shallow and unsatisfactory.

So I came away convinced that generalizations can be made about our friendships—based on our common experience as humans, as Americans, as members of particular economic, ethnic, and other groups—but that the real surprises come when we dig beneath the surface of the sweeping generalization to see what it is that's going on with us. We are more complex than we think.

Fourth: When I began to research this book on the meaning of friendship in our lives as people and as Americans, I assumed I would work up a set of standards—a definition, as it were—of friendship. As it turned out, that intention was, if not presumptuous, at least naïve. There is no magic formula for friendship that works for us all; we have our common humanity but we live our lives idiosyncratically.

Certainly there are some characteristics most of us—six or sixty, hippies or factory workers or shopkeepers—expect from our friends. We want to be able to trust our friends, feel that they are honest with us in terms of our relationship, feel they accept us—in the sense of "You're okay by me." We expect to enjoy our friends, to have an exchange of warmth suffusing the relationship, and—whether we articulate it or are even aware of it—we expect them to fill a bundle of needs.

Beyond that, things become ambiguous, the ingredients for the formula less pat. Good friends see each other more or less regularly? Some friendships ripen and deepen via the exchange of letters. And quite a few of us have the capacity to keep intact—

even to allow to flourish—friendships with friends who are no longer in close geographical proximity to us.

Good friends enjoy each other in a variety of different ways? Some very intense friendships can develop between people who have intense interests in common: chess friends, for instance, or colleague friends absorbed in a fascinating scientific research project.

Good friends drop masks, are open with each other? Well, from early childhood we learn that the difference between close friends and the other kind is that we can "share secrets" with the close ones. And it is certainly true that we are more relaxed, and therefore less guarded, with the friends we trust most. But I did not come away convinced that "baring our souls" is necessarily synonymous with the opening of our hearts to others: some people, though able to give and receive the warmth of friendship, simply will not talk—or talk only fleetingly—about certain aspects of themselves, such as their marriages or sex problems; some others compulsively spill it all out, to near-strangers as well as to close friends. Few of us would say that the latter persons are prime candidates for excellence in friendship. And what about vigorous intellectual friendships? When two people derive joy from the way they stimulate the flow of ideas in each other, from the way they spur each other on to leaps of the imagination, is their relationship necessarily less imbued with warmth and affection than one in which a lot of intimate revelations are made? That's really hard to believe; we give of ourselves in many different ways, in ways individually appropriate to us.

This brings me to my final point: how much we vary, each from the other, in our capacity for closeness, our ability to be open, our need for friendship (though I came away from the research convinced as never before that we all need it to some degree). Describing their friendships to me, some people called them "close," though from my personal perspective I saw them as superficial. In time I realized how irrelevant my reaction was in relation to what was actually going on with *them*. To be sure, some wished for closer friendship and were distressed about this lack in their lives. But others were involved in as much closeness as they wanted to be involved in and could tolerate. Their version of closeness may not be my version or your version—but it is real and meaningful to them.

So I came to believe that closeness is a relative value, not an absolute one, and that in the final analysis no one can define our friendships for us. We must, all of us, do that for ourselves—based on our awareness of ourselves, of our needs, and of the ways our friendships work in our lives. Essentially, that's what this book is all about.

2

Societal Strains and Pressures

NO question that in the United States friendship, along with God and motherhood, is a value that is Good. Making sure their youngsters have friends is a routine child-rearing function, and some parents rush for professional help if their children show any signs of being loners. People commonly refer to neighborhoods and communities as "friendly" and "unfriendly," depending on the openness of the residents. The advertising industry knows a good selling gimmick when it sees one; like pretty girls, the idea of friendship sells. It has been used to sell travel, soap, dandruff shampoo, gargles, and bourbon; in New York City a famous bank has a famous slogan: "You have a friend at Chase Manhattan." And Dale Carnegie's famous *How to Win Friends and Influence People*, written in 1936, has gone through ninety-five printings and sold over 7,500,000 copies—and is a hot item on the paperback racks even now.

That a book dealing in large part with the art of making and using friends could be so popular says at least three things about the society that keeps it everlastingly in print: one, the people of that society want friends—or at least want the feeling that they are liked; two, they think that rules for the winning of friends and the conduct of friendship can be prescribed in a book (they cannot); three, they find it hard to make or keep friends—or, maybe, to manage the friendships they do have.

To a certain extent problems related to friendships are rooted in the personalities of the people involved, but of course our personalities are significantly shaped by our social and personal environments. In this chapter let us consider several major facets of the social environment—of our society—that to greater or lesser degree affect us all in the conduct of our friendships. Specifically, we will be looking at the lack of societal ground rules in the conduct of our friendships, at the influence of money, at socioeconomic and geographical mobility, at competition, and at romantic love. The following two chapters will consider other influences upon us in relation to our friendships—the profound effect of our evolutionary history, and the societal and psychological needs that friendship satisfies and that therefore give to this relationship a predetermined quality.

Making, keeping, and interacting with friends would be easiest, of course, if we lived in a society where friendships are highly organized, highly institutionalized. In the patterning of friendships we have little in common with the peasants of Banoi, a village in central Thailand, where friendship commitments are "to the death." Or with the Tangu of New Guinea, whose mores forbid friendships between men and women or between two people of either sex whose age differences could place them in a parent-child relationship; whose mores forbid, too, friends to walk around as "couples" or to act together as a unit. Where friendships are so rigidly organized, every friend knows the rules, knows his friendship role.

We would chafe under rules and restrictions. As anthropologist Robert Paine has pointed out, we are under the thumb of an "efficient and dispassionate" bureaucracy that regulates our other relationships, and it is one of the charming attractions of our unstructured friendships that they remain unstructured in comparison with the other relationships we are involved in daily. I'm thinking of Ron, whom I see but once a year in warm reunions.

Could I sit with Ron and a bottle of scotch for half the night, both of us catching up on events—and on our relationship—if there were cultural laws forcing us to do so? Possibly I could and would if that was how my culture conditioned me—or I might find ways of evading those laws, something that also sometimes happens in societies where friendships are rigidly structured.

Still, I recoil at the thought of *having* to be with—and to behave in a certain way with—a close friend. Most of us would, I think, opt for the kind of society we live in now, where we have the freedom to conduct our friendships as we please.

Freedom is a double-edged blade: it slices us free of restrictions but it also cuts us off from the comfort and security of knowing exactly what is expected of us and how we should behave with our friends. Unlike members of primitive societies, we make up our friendship rules as we go along. We make decisions relating to our friendships—and there are a lot of decisions to make—as we go along. Decisions such as these: how open we can be with this person, how far to commit ourselves in that relationship, whether to encourage a potential new friendship, how much time to give this friend or that.

We do not necessarily spend hours mulling over these or other points; at times we make those decisions almost automatically; but we are under pressure to make them. At times the pressure (added to all the other pressures we are subject to) can be quite burdensome. When it gets to be too much we show it, even those of us who are normally gregarious and accustomed to reaching out, by retreating from friends for a bit. We need a rest.

Money may or may not be the root of all evil, but it surely is a basis for many friendship decisions. The allocation of time given to friends has to do with how much time you *want* to spend with them but also with how much you *can* spend with them. What is quaintly called gainful employment eats up a lot of available time for both men and women—as do other activities related to economics, such as the running of a household.

The seventy-hour-a-week executive has very little chance to socialize in the conventional sense (and may wish to keep his friendships superficial). The assembly-line worker, especially in automobile plants, where the pressure is excruciating, comes home too pooped to think of getting together with anybody; what with overtime and everything, drinking a couple of beers and watching some television is about all he can manage.

Lots of people these days work at two jobs, which certainly leaves hardly any time for socializing. John G. Theban, executive director of Family and Child Services in Washington, D.C., sees at first hand how this phenomenon can cause family tensions centered around friendships. With many of the families that come in for counseling, almost all of them black and most of them poor, this is the pattern that emerges: the husband works hard at two jobs to improve the family's material lot. He has no time or energy left over to help develop family friendships. His wife feels isolated and becomes resentful. Next she begins to develop her own social outlets, both same-sex and opposite-sex. This makes the husband resentful, for he feels that she should simply appreciate what he is doing and not make any demands on him. A marital rift develops.

The kinds of friends one chooses are also very much bound up with money—more specifically, with socioeconomic status. Studies of friendship patterns in the United States are unanimous in concluding that birds of a class stick together, at least when they are grown-up birds. Middle-class and lower-class children do play together and cement friendships when they are in elementary school, but as they grow older the cement crumbles; interests diverge and the incongruence in life-styles becomes ever more intrusive.

This is a sad but familiar scene, the drifting apart of children who, when younger, embodied the melting-pot ideal in their relationships. Very few of the adults who spoke to me about their friendships anywhere in the country reported striking differences in a socioeconomic sense between themselves and their friends. One significant exception: a minority of middle-class men and women reported having very *rich* friends. (Frankly, I didn't talk to enough really wealthy people to get a sense of how they defined their middle-class friends.) Hardly any middle-class person I talked to could point to a working-class friend, and the exceptions stick in my mind. A couple of notable ones follow:

. . . A lady in Brooklyn, New York. Her husband is an academician and she numbers among the friends who mean a good deal to her a lady whose husband is a mechanic. They became acquainted at Ethical Culture Society meetings. "There's a real bond; if we needed each other we'd come through, I guess. But we never discuss our intimate problems—and we both have them, believe me. I don't understand how she can stand her husband, she doesn't understand how anybody could get a divorce. In terms of children, schools, social action, we're really tuned in to each other but we don't understand each other's family structure. I don't think she really understands the options open to me, to women, to children when they grow up. . . ." Though they live in the same neighborhood, their worlds outside Ethical Culture rarely if ever converge; their husbands never, *never* meet.

. . . A translator in Los Angeles whose civil libertarian zeal is passionate. He reports having had a long and very rewarding friendship with a Sicilian auto mechanic; what brought them together was their love for fine racing cars. But that was years ago, and the translator has moved about a good deal, both here and in Europe. It has been a matter of occasionally forging close relationships, as with the Sicilian mechanic, then having to endure separations. Most striking was this: the translator had kept up a voluminous correspondence with other friends from whom he is now separated, all of his own social class. Yet though he is fluent in Italian, he and the Sicilian have not exchanged a word in years. Out of cars, out of mind.

One might assume that liberals would be most apt to have at least a sprinkling of lower-class friends—well, I, at least, could detect no flaming urge on the part of liberals to cultivate such friends. A lawyer heavily involved in Democratic politics told me, "It would be embarrassing to be with someone poor. We couldn't go to the same places, do the same things. . . ." His wife rather wistfully referred to a poor but well-educated couple they know. "They're likable people but my husband doesn't enjoy visiting them because their surroundings make him feel uncomfortable."

Social mobility—getting up in the world or getting down in the world—often really has a profound effect on one's old friendships. Improving one's lot in life, especially, can be the death of a relationship. Typically, the upward climb means higher earnings and a gradual if not sudden change in one's life-style—a move to more expensive surroundings, perhaps, a different set of friends, more stylish living in general. Bit by bit old friends fade away. People often swear otherwise when good fortune strikes—"Pete and Mary, things will always be the same between us"—and it is meant with utter sincerity but does not often work out that way, at least not in the long run. And in some cases the promotion of an executive to a higher organizational level results in the deliberate severing of friendships with nice people who are now subordinates instead of colleagues.

All this can be very wrenching, but the drastic effect on friendship is there nonetheless. Downward social mobility—demotion, loss of job, whatever—can of course have the same effect. In some cases the target of ill fortune himself withdraws from his friends, as if ashamed. He *is* ashamed, for it isn't in his ability to love his wife or be a dedicated parent or a devoted friend upon which he has based his identity—it is primarily in his ability to provide and provide well that he gains his sense of self-esteem.

Geographical mobility is sometimes fueled by social mobility, sometimes not. Social critics who wish to point to the decline of American life in general or of American friendships in particular often point to our propensity for moving; in their thesis is an important element of proof. As they say, one family in five pulls up stakes and moves to another residence each year; some corporations move their executives every couple of years or so; and military families are notorious for the amount of moving they are subject to. In the good old days, critics like Vance Packard say or imply, it was not this way at all. In his hand-wringing *A Nation of Strangers*, for instance, Packard tries to show that transiency is responsible for everything from the deterioration of relationships to pathology of all kinds—including perhaps alcoholism, disorientation, cancer, coronary disease, and more.

It seems to me we have enough social problems without overstating any of them; it might be helpful to bring some perspective to bear on geographical mobility. There is no arguing the point that we are very transient, but the observation calls for a lot of amplification. For one thing, as Columbia University sociologist Herbert Gans points out, "most of the 20 per cent of Americans who move every year only change dwellings in the same neighborhood" and presumably keep the same friends. Not much more than a third of the moving population moves across a country or state line.

And it was ever thus. Witness the westward migration, and the flood of immigrants to the United States, great waves of people rolling across the American landscape. Look at the surprising results of nineteenth-century population studies, such as those collected by Yale University: Boston, 1830–60, with an annual population turnover of at least 30 per cent—more than the current national rate; Poughkeepsie, N.Y., 1850–80, "with a constant reshuffling of the majority of residents on most streets" year after year. Then there are in-depth social anthropological studies of "typical" American towns—such as Warner and Lunt's famous profile of "Yankee City," an anonymous New England industrial town of about 17,000 where, in the 1930s, all the young men kept leaving to find richer opportunities in the bigger cities. Certain styles in relation to mobility may be different now, such as the classes of people who move and the number of times each family moves in its particular lifetime—but Americans were never a sedentary group.

What's important here is not the number of times a person moves but the impact of mobility on relationships in general and friendships in particular. To this point, it is hard to find an easy answer. How can we speak of geographical mobility that affects everyone equally when in fact moving from one place to another means different things to different people in different situations? The emotions of the wife who faces relocation because her husband is being transferred yet again by his organization may be quite different from those of the wife whose family, after prolonged soul-searching, decides it is time to move to the suburbs. The implications of a move are clearly different for the older person who buys a condominium in an expensive retirement community and the older person who must check into an old-age home. The expectations and anxieties of the child bussed to a different school every few years due to the requirements of racial balance may be unlike those of the child whose parents pull up stakes and move to another city where work opportunities are greater.

In fact, a new dimension in terms of American mobility

patterns has come into being as a result of school bussing to correct racial imbalance in the schools; periodically, then, friendships are broken and new ones form. Friendship disruptions, too, occur in the lives of poor people forced to relocate because of massive urban renewal programs.

Do friendships live or die when there is a move? Do friends somehow remain incorporated in each other's lives? If it depends on the people involved, are there patterns to suggest who will respond one way and who the other? Later chapters will explore these questions, as well as the more profound one of whether repeated moves cause subtle but permanent personality changes in an individual. Some observers suggest they do—in the direction of less trust, less ability to show affection, more depersonalization—though these observations often are based on studies of troubled people. Suffice it to say here that geographical mobility causes some people to withdraw in a sense, some others to shape meaningful friendships in a less traditional way. Geographical mobility does not allow easy generalizations, except for the obvious one that its impact on friendship patterns is signficant, always.

A pressure that affects friendships of all kinds in all situations is competition. As human beings we have within us urges both competitive and cooperative; as Americans we are subject to the strong competitive force of our particular society. No matter what social atmosphere they are raised in, no matter how cooperative, children show elements of competition in their free play and are subject to some competitive forces; this holds true even in the kibbutzim of Israel, where competition is philosophically disavowed. Even societies that extoll cooperation to the point of making competition practically a taboo—for instance, the gentle mountain-dwelling Arapesh made famous by Margaret Mead—embody some competitive exchanges. So in America, where winning has always had something mystical about it (how many people *really* believe it's how you play the game, not whether you win, that really counts?), competition is a mighty powerful force, both in international and in personal affairs. No less so, by the way, when marked by seeming passivity or acquiescence.

Youngsters, especially middle-class youngsters, learn from a very early age that it is better to do better than the others—to get the better grades, win the Little League games, become popular (more popular than the others; after all, if everyone received equal approval the coin of popularity would be devalued), wear the most appropriate clothes (whether good or shabby or good *and* shabby), and otherwise excel.

Recoiling from this pressure as they grow older, some teen-agers bewilder their parents by withdrawing from the competition. But many dropouts, even, have not shed the competition they so desperately want to abjure: they have a strong, strong need to affirm *their* specialness. For the rest, competition becomes stiffer—in high school and certainly in most colleges. At Georgetown University, where academics and intelligence are stressed, a male student acknowledged, "My relationships are competitive because *I'm* competitive," and, in an apparent effort to soft-pedal the rough-and-tumble sound of this remark, added, "But all our cards are on the table, we all have equal power. It's up to each of us then to take what's equal between us and try to achieve from that point."

If that does not exactly have an easy ring to it, the reason may well be that nothing about adolescent competition is easy: this is the time when friends are dear, maybe dearer than they will ever again be—but this also happens to be the time one is in direct competition with one's friends.

Generalized competition, always flavoring the American at-mosphere, exacerbates the competitive element in relationships that are uneasy in any event: between the sexes, for instance, and between the generations. Whether in very soft focus, then, or sharply defined, competition is in the grain of American friend-ships (but certainly not only American friendships; it was the great French aphorist La Rochefoucauld back in the seventeenth century who said, "In the misfortunes of our dearest friends we always find something not entirely displeasing"). Not infrequently with groups of males and females a discussion of friendship sparks spirited debate as to whether women or men are more competitive in their same-sex friendships, but rarely if ever did I hear anyone make claim that competition is entirely lacking.

How much competition exists between any two individuals

depends on how competitive each of them is essentially, of course, as well as on their behavioral styles and on the substance of their bond. The competition can be so mild it hardly seems an element in the relationship, and only occasionally asserts itself in word, deed, or flashing thought. Highly competitive people are something else again: their style always includes one-upmanship and they hardly ever completely stop playing the power game with those individuals who make them feel most competitive. They play it as though being brainy or skillful or clever or witty or such is the scarcest goods in the world. While a dash of competition can spice up a relationship, when used heavy-handedly it wards off real closeness and intimacy. Which may be one of the reasons some people *are* so heavy-handed with it.

As most men and women grow into adulthood, though, they instinctively protect themselves from the more corrosive effects of competition. One striking way is to avoid making friends with people with whom they are already competitively involved. This is as true of factory workers as it is of corporation men; when sociologist Edward Gross took a close look at eleven informal groups of friends in the head office of a Chicago manufacturing and mail-order firm, he failed to find a single pair of friends whose situation in the work place was remotely competitive. Women whose backgrounds were so similar and who had so much in common that they could be expected to be the greatest of friends did not establish a bond at all—and Gross discovered that in each such case the women were working for the same boss or otherwise competitively involved in terms of their occupation.

It is not enough in friendship to choose persons we like; too, we have to feel that they will not directly threaten us. And though we can't always defend against this threat—and may not in every instance even wish to do so—in the main we try very hard. Understandably, we do not want the tensions, the conflicts, the hurts that potentially exist. We don't want to have to tussle with our consciences in what may be a tug-of-war between what is good for our friends and what is good for us.

There is a tug-of-war of sorts between institutions—the one of friendship and the one of marriage. Ideally, the outside friendships that a husband and wife have enhance their marriage, and the joy and warmth they find in their marriage enrich their friendship bonds. But in the real world of men and women outside friendships can, and far from occasionally do, have a destructive rather than a constructive effect on marriage.

In fact, the traditional fabric of American love and marriage, spun from romantic love, is prone to rips and tears because of competition arising from close outside friendships on the part of either partner. Romantic love is exclusive love, mysterious love, powerful-force love, you-render-me-helpless love, you're-the-only-one-for-me kind of love. In its ultimate state the romantic lovers' world is seen as being without doors or windows to the outside, for the lovers are everything to each other and fill each other's every need. If we are everything to each other, my beloved and I, what need do we have for the intimacy of close friendship? Romantic love is possessive love, and possessive love creates what Germaine Greer has called "the symbiosis of mutual dependence" in which each is the other's only true, true friend.

I don't mean to suggest that most couples engage in a lifelong career of being everything to each other (although a few do), or that in this day and age most people actually embrace the tenets of romantic love with intellectual as well as emotional fervor. Yet the illusions, the expectations, the fantasies, the utopian daydreams triggered by this kind of love are very much with us still, both among the young and the not-so-young. Dr. Jetse Sprey, a sociologist at Case Western Reserve University in Cleveland, says that when he talks to students about the "inhumanness" of the modern symbiotic marriage, those students respond, "Yes, but in our case it's going to be different, we'll make it work." When family-service agencies counsel troubled families around the issue of friendships, the most common refrain social workers hear is, "He spends too much time with the boys" (and now, more often, "She's out with the girls too much")—issues that center around the feeling of being left out.

As for marriages in general, especially middle-class ones, the predominant pattern seems to be for couples to have friendships with other couples. When friends do visit each other on an individual basis, it's most often over lunch or around work or organizational activities. That is, in situations that do not take one away from one's mate. In many places community mores are a factor, too, in dictating how little or how much time a person can spend with friends alone. Often more rights are conferred upon one partner—usually the man—than upon the other.

"I see friends mostly on a couple-to-couple basis because the area in which we live does not provide social approval for married women acting 'singly,'" observed Sally, a young wife living in a small community near San Diego, California. Sally did add that the women's movement has had the effect of "bestowing some sort of legitimacy on 'the girls' getting together. This community is dominated by the male ethic—how he likes his beer and how he likes his women."

The pressures upon Sally are unique to her and her environment, of course, but they serve as a reminder that all of us in our relationships with friends are influenced by the forces of society. Onerous as ours may seem at times, we should not forget that each environment, each society, has pressures unique to it, restricting friendships in one way, enchancing them in another. We pursue our connections as people everywhere have always done, some of us falteringly, some of us with sureness and joy—all of us influenced not only by social forces but also by other kinds of forces that reach from a dimly perceived past to a startling present.

3

Programed for Friendship

FRIENDSHIP is a relationship that has endured and persisted throughout the span of human history. When I'm playing chess with a friend or having drinks with a friend there are (if I stop to think about it) echoes: of the aborigines of a few thousand years ago squatting on their haunches with their friends, engaged in exchanges peculiar to their day; of Greeks and Romans and their friends; of Elizabethans and their friends; of friends all along the road of time—strangers becoming less strange to each other, becoming closer, bonding.

Is the desire for friendship an innate characteristic? Are there societal impositions welding us into our friendship networks? Are there temperamental imperatives that, to greater or lesser degree, influence us toward the formation of friendships? Obviously, we can only conjecture, but such conjecture can be more than merely fascinating—it can help us to see our friendships more clearly and, ultimately, ourselves more sharply.

When and how does friendship begin? Many psychologists and some ethologists are convinced that the relationship between infant and mother (or surrogate mother) is really the starting point for the relationship between friends. The newborn child arrives in the alien world not as alien as it might at first glance appear. Evolution has provided it with many skills, has programed it for survival. It can grasp. It can cling. It can suck. It can scream for food.

The child feeds, the mother cuddles the feeding child, the screams quiet down. Impressed by this ineluctable drama, Freud concluded that each of us learns to love because of our need for food—learns, so early in life, to attach ourselves to another human being and from that one to others, in an ever-widening network of associations. Is friendship simply a matter of food-related learning, then? It would seem not. As the German ethologist Irenaus Eibl-Eibesfeld points out, when we are infants we scream not only for food. We do so when we are wet or otherwise uncomfortable. We do so when we want some attention paid to us. Even the youngest babies sometimes scream for no apparent reason—but calm down very quickly when picked up, cuddled, snuggled, or baby-talked to. What does this mean? That they already want to be picked up, cuddled, snuggled, and baby-talked to—that they seem born with this need.

Even when they are as young as six months of age, many babies can distinguish between friends (knowns) and strangers (unknowns)—and between a "special" friend (person) among a host of friendly persons. Even young babies can exhibit behavior instantly recognizable as "friendly"—gurgling, kicking their legs in glee, smiling. The smile is a peculiarly human characteristic; no animal can smile. But wherever a baby smiles—in a California split-level, a Peruvian jungle hut, an Alaskan igloo—that smile is instantly recognizable in the same way: those seeing the smile know instantly that the baby is making friendly contact with the world.

From these and other observations Eibl-Eibesfeld concludes that we are all programed to connect with our environment, we are all born with an "appetite" for contact. In short, our evolutionary history has provided us with this talent.

Why should it have done so? Much has to do with our physical vulnerabilities. As our Paleolithic ancestors already knew, we cannot make it alone. The occasional hermit is able to exist only because he *is* occasional, and because by and large the environment in which he lives by himself has already been tamed by nonhermits. The vast majority of us have had, from our earliest days, to live in groups—so as to tame harsh environments, build shelter, provide ourselves with food and protection, to satisfy the most elemental physical needs. If we were to live in groups we had to develop the mechanisms that would enable us to do so—to curb indiscriminate aggression. The feeling of "we"—the friendly "we" —against "them"—the unfriendly, potentially hostile, or outrightly dangerous "them"—is such a mechanism. Konrad Lorenz has reasonably proposed that our aggressive instincts have been vital to the preservation of the species. Then friendly feelings, precursors of actual friendships, must have been equally vital. Else the members of each group would have fallen upon each other as casually as misdirected self-interest might prompt, and the groups so necessary for survival could themselves not have survived.

However it was for our ancestors in prehistoric times, the distinctions between friendship to enhance group membership and group membership as a way of facilitating friendships are blurred for us, I think. Several years a number of us, parents on Manhattan's West Side, felt compelled to band together in response to an ugly set of circumstances surrounding our children's public schools. Our shared mission made comrades out of strangers; not only were we working together, we felt ourselves linked by an invisible chain of sympathy and understanding. Many of us remarked on the beautiful thing that was happening to us, and soon this experience as much as our common goal held us together. We saw far more of each other than we did our long-standing friends on the "outside." Once the emergency was over, personality differences that had been disregarded asserted themselves, and there were fights and fallings-out among us; the group fell apart. But some of us still number close friends from among those spirited days.

Our pattern was hardly unique to us. In early 1969, for instance, Harvard sociologist Michael Useem interviewed nearly a hundred draft resisters in the Boston area. Most said the same thing: many friendships with persons not in the resistance movement lessened, sometimes collapsed altogether. The more access these young people had to others in the movement, the more friendships they cemented within the movement. Many reported "an 'exhilarating feeling' of solidarity with the community of resisters . . . a spirit of common cause prevailed, and an instinctive warmth was felt by all who had resisted."

Not only is friendship a survival mechanism when viewed in relation to the species as a whole, it serves clear and distinct functions in each society where it is practiced. In many primitive societies, friends must meet specific qualifications in order to become friends and follow stringent rules in order to continue the friendship. Seemingly arbitrary, these qualifications and rules really are not: they have evolved with a remarkable internal logic that makes friendship a tool in the maintenance of each such society. Anthropologist S. N. Einsenstadt has taken note of this in connection with "particularistic" societies—those where allegiance to one's group (based on age, caste, etc.) is much stronger than allegiance to the society as a whole. Friendships between members of the differing groups, he says, hold the larger society together, keep it from splintering. In other primitive societies friendships offer a way to economic betterment or provide havens in a hazardous environment. Members of the Zande tribe in Africa, for instance, become blood brothers with members of another tribe, so that they will have friends when traveling in possibly hostile country.

For us, too, friendships play important societal roles, link us in crucial ways to our society. Imagine a world in which friendship as both concept and actuality vanished. There would be no nonfamily people to talk with, to share with, to be close to. Many of us would feel emotionally deprived, of course, but we would also suffer the loss of a very important channel of communication. For us no less than for the primitive, daily life becomes easier, smoother, perhaps even more possible, because of the informational exchanges that occur between ourselves and our friends. All the more so if our families are small and no relatives live nearby.

In a world without friends we would have no one outside our families or the occasional cab driver or hairdresser or bartender with whom to talk about the more personal facets of our lives—and we may not always choose to talk about such things to our families or a cab driver or hairdresser or bartender. Child-rearing instruction does not come our way solely by courtesy of Dr. Spock or Dr. Ginnott—we pick up much of it from conversations with friends. Lacking friends we would have a much harder time than we now do in checking our perceptions as parents and in evaluating our children's progress.

Without friends the pool of persons with whom we now share viewpoints on movies, television shows, sports, politics, and such would be greatly diminished. Work friends would not exist, and we would be deprived of office or shop talk—the easy talk that lets us know what's going on, where we stand, what management's expectations are, who's out of favor and why, what we can get away with and what we can't; we would be deprived of people to help and be helped by in the work situation, and of people to relax with there. Going on vacation or moving to another area would be rendered much more difficult; there would be so few people around us who had been there, or knew others who had been there, and could give us the benefit of gossip, hearsay, or experience.

We think of gossip negatively—in the context, say, of two people talking about a third behind his back. Actually, gossip means the transmission of rumor, reports, *and* behind-the-scenes information. In this sense gossip helps us to orient ourselves to community standards. Through it we learn over and over again what is expected of us and why; it is a form of social control.

When, for instance, Mrs. Brody tells Mrs. Parker that Mrs. Lewis down the street has been secretly swilling the Cold Duck again, Mrs. Brody is doing more than just telling Mrs. Parker about somebody else's weakness; she is saying, "We don't approve of that kind of thing around here; I don't expect you to act that way." When Mr. Thomas tells his friend Mr. Edwards about how another friend had lost a bundle in a stock-market deal, Mr. Edwards gains information invaluable to him in his own stock-market transactions—and through the friend of a friend he does not even know. Much of our information comes to us like that, like a torch passed from hand to hand, sometimes from far away, always to illuminate our paths in life. In at least one society—on the West Indian island of St. Vincent—gossip is institutionalized. Friends must gossip with and about each other. There gossip clearly is used both as a form of communication and as a means of societal control; it helps regulate behavior, for it embarrasses people to be gossiped about.

We operate in the societal realm; we operate in the psychological realm; we have emotional wants and needs to be gratified. In the latter instance, too, friendships play their important parts—important enough to give a feeling of inevitability about this particular relationship. Who can really tell whether the earliest humans, banding together in friendly groups, derived the kind of emotional gratifications from their relationships that we associate with our good friendships? It may be, as Konrad Lorenz suggests, that a rudimentary kind of affection and satisfaction passed between Cro-Magnon man and his friends. It may be that something deeper and more psychologically complex evolved over time. We do know that from nearly the earliest days of recorded history emotionally satisfying friendship was already a motif in the mythology of peoples: for instance, it was said of two ancient Egyptian gods, Ra and Osiris, that they "each embraced the other and they became as one soul in two souls"; in the mythology of ancient India it was said of two divine friends, "The heart of Vishnu is Siva, and the heart of Siva is Vishnu." We also know—so the anthropologists tell us—that even in those primitive tribes where friendship is highly institutionalized, and therefore highly functional, the relationship between close friends is characterized by strong emotional bonds.

Whatever other functions friendship serves for us in our time, the psychological dimension is obviously the crucial one between ourselves and our friends. We cannot gain all of our gratifications from our relationships with lovers, spouses, parents, or children. When we try we become locked inside tight little boxes that exclude the world and eventually suffocate one or all, but there are other considerations. Being looser, freer, not bound by the same moral, legal, or familiar considerations that these other relationships are bound by, our friendships don't require as much role-playing on our part; we can give freer rein to our personalities—or to more facets of our personalities. Since we are not bound to our friends by ties other than those we choose to form, our friendships are continual (if subliminal) reminders that we are worthy, that we are important, that we have been singled out for ourselves. This can make it easier to drop masks, to be ourselves, to expose our weaknesses as well as our strengths.

Friends help us to accept ourselves, reinforce our values, mitigate our aloneness generally as humans and specifically in terms of our thoughts and feelings ("If my friend feels as I do, I can't be so alone and different"). When we are young, friends help us to separate from our families of origin; when we are older they act as buffers between ourselves and our acquired families, helping to reduce the emotional strain that comes with close family living.

All these elements need amplification and qualification; many of the chapters to come will concern themselves in part with the psychological workings of our friendships. The point here is that our friendships are not ancillary relationships, secondary relationships; they serve very specific emotional needs—as is borne out by the effects of isolation.

It is common knowledge that isolates in rooming houses and gloomy hotel rooms are high-risk candidates for mental illness. A study of isolated farmers and ranchers in rural Montana shows that they are no better off; despite the romanticization of the "plains people," a sociological study has found them domineering and selfish, and has pinpointed a marked association between the isolated outdoor life and mental illness. Seclusiveness is a marked trait among many schizophrenics—and if they are not wholly withdrawn their friendships are nonetheless marked by a noticeable absence of depth; one researcher notes that some young preschizophrenics are saved from becoming full-blown ones by "the buffer of a close relationship with a friend." A massive study of urban residents—the Midtown Manhattan study of 1954, involving 1660 men, women, and children—confirms the association between friendship and mental health: a very high risk of *poor* mental health is associated with the absence of close friends. Interestingly, the number of neighbors the interviewees were friendly with, and the number of organizations they belonged to were only moderately associated with sound mental functioning. Friendships played a much more important role.

Thus, our ties to friends count for much more in our lives than we might realize. From the standpoint of our evolutionary history, the functioning of our societies, and our own psychological requirements, friendship is a relationship that "had to be."

4

Friendship and Intimacy

IT is said that we can't like others unless we first like ourselves. It is said that we can't enjoy other people's company unless we first enjoy our own. It is said that we are better off staying by ourselves than being friends with people we do not fully respect.

Such truisms have a nice ring, but life has a way of tempering if not flatly contradicting them. Even if we are not wholly enchanted with ourselves we manage to strike up friendships; the very fact that others like us makes us like ourselves better. Even if we are reasonably self-sufficient we sometimes find ourselves in situations in which the pool of potential friends is small and consequently become involved with people we would not ordinarily choose.

Some contact, we finally conclude, is better than no contact at all. An American woman who, with her husband, lived in an underdeveloped African country for several years told me how difficult it was to be accepted into its society; foreigners were forced to be only with each other. "I met people I wouldn't think of striking up friendships with here because of certain characteristics that turned me off," she said. "But the longer I stayed there the less important all that became. At first I deliberately overlooked things, then they didn't register so much because we became like one big family." Once back in the United States she met a few members of the "family" and found herself reacting to their negative qualities; she was no longer under the compulsion to make friends among a very limited group of individuals. She had compromised in Africa because of her need for people.

We all need people. We are all born with that "appetite" for contact. How much of an appetite—the extent to which we can and do reach out to others—is an individual matter depending on a host of circumstances. "It is often temperament that makes men brave and women chaste," remarked the irresistible La Rochefoucald, and it is also temperament that in part determines our ability to get close to people. All babies smile, but not every baby smiles with the same degree of warmth or the same constancy. The very youngest infants are much more than innocuous blobs just waiting for life experiences to shape them into definite personalities. The youngest of us already possesses a distinct temperament. There has been such a focus on the environmental influences upon behavior, both in the scientific and popular literature, that this fact is frequently disregarded.

For more than a decade and a half, Dr. Stella Chess of New York University along with several colleagues has studied the origins of personality. They have followed the development of well over two hundred boys and girls from infancy on, concluding that most babies fall into three temperamental categories. Some—40 per cent of the study group—have sunny, friendly dispositions. Others—some 15 per cent—are cautious types, slow to warm up to people and to adapt to new experiences. Still others—about 10 per cent—are "difficult" children—prone to temper tantrums, bossy, warding off rather than welcoming people, at least initially. (About a third of the group defied easy categorization.) These were the "styles" the babies brought with them into the world. Other researchers have also been working on, and finding, distinct temperaments in babies. Obviously, even the youngest infant is subject to environmental influences—for instance, the way it is delivered, the way it is first handled—but it does not emerge from the womb with nothing in the way of innate traits.

Of course, our temperaments do not live in a vaccuum; they grow and flourish and alter in contact with the environments they are exposed to, the life experiences we encounter. In a rare psychoanalytic paper on friendship, analyst Leo Rangell points out that friendly feelings are awakened in us by the first person to allay our anxieties—usually our mother or mother-substitutes.

The experience of being mothered is our first; contact quickly follows with father, siblings, and other family members. Often in the backgrounds of men and women who are prone to keep distance between themselves and others were absent or rejecting mothers or fathers—early emotional deprivation that led them to be cautious in relating to other people. Rejection breeds rejection: we frequently protect ourselves from hurt by using the very style that brought on the hurt—frequently, but certainly not always. There are people whose history of emotional deprivation leads them to a desperate lifelong search for nurturing friends and lovers; they expect friends and lovers or mates to do the impossible job of making up for their earlier lacks; they cling to others. Paradoxically, their need for friends is so overwhelming that they drive potential friends away and remain friendless. The death of a parent early in life can—and not infrequently does—cause problems in relating. The overly possessive, smothering parent can frighten a child enough to have it run from closeness.

And yet there are men and women who somehow confound psychological theories or observation by emerging unscathed from emotionally deprived or unhealthy childhoods, who become well able to form close, loving relationships with the significant persons in their lives. Maybe they were temperamentally so inclined, maybe initially good experiences with other relatives and first friends has taught them to be trusting.

I don't mean to suggest that only temperament and early childhood experiences are significant, that later experiences with friends and others count for naught. Of course, disillusioning experiences with friends in adult life can shatter our sense of trust, can serve to distance us from others to the point where, as a Chicago secretary in her early thirties poignantly expressed it, "I'll never have a close friend again." But if friends hurt us badly over and over again, we are forced to ask ourselves why we choose such friends, and then too the painful path backward for a search of the reasons generally brings us again to our youth.

To refer to people as being "close" to others or as "distancing" themselves from others is in a sense misleading. We have our predominant styles and characteristics, but to view ourselves—or to be viewed—only in those terms is too simplistic. We may not contain Walt Whitman's multitudes, but we are certainly not only that which we seem to be on the surface. This is very evident in relation to friendship and intimacy.

When I interviewed working-class men in formal settings the image they usually presented was conventionally masculine—strong, tough, self-contained, little emotion showing through. When I interviewed similar men in more relaxed settings—for instance, having drinks with them at veterans' posts—many became freer about revealing their feelings, and certainly much less unemotional. "I love this guy, I really do!" exuberantly cried a telephone company lineman at a V.F.W. post near Boston after he had introduced me to his buddy for the third time. He had been there for hours and he was bleary-eyed, but it was clear he meant what he said, especially when he added, "But you know, not, like, in an effeminate way."

These men were affectionate with their friends, too—showing them off to me with evident pride; kidding, clowning, bear-hugging them, being physical with them in the kind of way men are when they want to be demonstrative with each other but also reassure the world about their masculinity.

When I interviewed businessmen, however, either formally or informally, a different pattern seemed to emerge: these men generally were guarded about their feelings while sober, and for the most part they were guarded about their feelings after having had a few drinks. They conformed to the image of the close-mouthed executive.

If one wants to make a case for stereotyping management types as compulsive, hard-driving men whose relationship with family and friends are very shallow, there is no end of proof to back one up. A *Harvard Business Review* study of forty American executives and their wives is eloquent in this respect. Hardly any of these men (average age, thirty-seven) acknowledged having feelings of dependence. Both husbands and wives said they made it a point to limit any feelings of tenderness in their younger children. Both placed a high premium on self-reliance. The men said it was very hard for them to admit to feeling tender or affectionate toward their friends. One man—who, oddly, called himself a "sentimentalist"—confessed to feeling embarrassed when his wife, addressing herself to some other people, referred to a friend of his as his "best friend."

In my own interviews I kept on hearing how difficult it is for high-level managers and entrepreneurs to form warm, relaxed friendships. A more competitive, emotionally controlled kind of person most often is drawn to, and makes a success of, the job; time demands are heavy, leaving little time for the pursuit of friendship; there is the competitiveness and concomitant suspiciousness generated by the setting: your colleague may be out for the position you are bucking for or currying favor with the boss, if not now then possibly later; your underlings might be out to take advantage of you, might be bucking for your job—and you, if you are too friendly with them, might lose your objectivity in making decisions that concern them.

Most executives, therefore, seem to make better friends with persons in organizations or professions other than their own. Better friends, yes, but still I kept on being told that a lot of those friendships are better described as "friendly relationships"—involving drinks, golf, cocktail parties, dinners at home for large crowds so no chance for real familiarity presents itself. Often, says Dr. Kenn Rogers, an expert in the psychology of businessmen, these are relationships based not only on linking but on mutual self-interest: "What can he do for me now, what might he be able to do for me later?"

Yet to say that executives by and large are guarded in their friendships—unwilling to reveal much of themselves, invest much of themselves, and/or derive much warmth from them—is to describe only predominant characteristics. There are managers who are as close to friends as they *can* be—which may not seem very close by somebody else's standards but satisfies their need in this respect. There are executives who are not close to others, don't know how to be close to others, and suffer on account of it; as Dr. Anthony J. Athos of the Harvard Business School notes, the executive role itself tends to generate loneliness. There are executives who, in their own ways, show a wish or a need for more open and trusting relationships: by cultivating certain people whose business potential is unlikely but who more conceivably might act as "listening posts" one day; by unburdening themselves to call girls; by using management consultants, who are called in to solve business problems, as "surrogate friends" in regard to personal problems.

Rarely are any of us so guarded, so closed in, that we keep our feelings completely locked inside ourselves. We reveal ourselves in subtle ways—by tones of voice, gestures, facial expressions, slips of the tongue, and the like, of course; but I'm not referring only to that kind of indirect communication. There are times in the life of even very self-protective, removed persons when emotions overflow, when joy or sorrow wells up too strongly to be contained. Then, unpredictably, there occur flashes of intimacy, of warmth or revelation. And they do occur in the lives of the high-level executives I explored: fleeting moments of openness over a drink on the way home from a meeting, on the eighteenth green, wherever—when emotion is strong and the time, though completely unplanned, is right. A lovely scene from the film *Save the Tiger* illustrates this point beautifully. A dress manufacturer has been providing an out-of-town buyer he has known for a long time with call girls whenever he comes to town. This time is no exception, but this time the buyer—moved by pain and shame—blurts it out: his wife has been an invalid for years and he desperately needs a woman once in a while. In that moment the buyer wanted to— needed to—say that he was more than a sex-hungry middle-aged man taking advantage of his power as a buyer; he wanted to be understood.

All of us, regardless of our capacity for intimacy, want to be understood.

Revealingly, the Harvard study of executives noted that a lot of the men felt more affection than they could show—but none intended to find ways of relating more openly and expressively.

Yet I didn't single out executives because they are necessarily so radically different from anybody else—only to show that even when people distance themselves from others as a way of life the appetite for contact shows up, now and again, in unexpected ways.

It can hardly be said that executives are unique in feeling more affection than they can show. That quirk seems to hold true for a great many of us. Some people say they love their friends, and described to me instances in which they and their particularly close friends were somehow moved to say so aloud to each other. As one might expect, almost all were women; it is still much easier for women to express such emotions aloud—for that matter, an occasional pleasantly high male blue-collar worker notwithstanding, it is easier for them even to acknowledge such emotions to themselves and others.

Most of us, men or women, are neither at the one extreme of remoteness nor at the other of committed lovingness in relation to our friends. Unlike social critics who see us only as shallow, I came away convinced that we are to be found at all points of intimacy from shallowness to warm affection to great love—that no one pattern fairly describes us. We are simply like people everywhere. In any event, love is a most difficult emotion to master —for us, for everyone; even Aristotle, who extolled love between friends, had to admit that only the rare person can love fully and skillfully.

All of us, no matter how secure or fearful we are in our relationships, find ways of achieving some distance between ourselves and others; in the happiest circumstances, we achieve the optimum psychic distance, where we feel the most comfortable and so do our friends. The "self-actualizers" studied by the late Dr. Abraham Maslow of Brandeis University—persons he felt represented the highest levels of mental health and personal fulfillment—are a striking case in point. Maslow described them as loving their friends, devoting much time to them, forming "more perfect identification . . . with them than other people would consider possible." Nevertheless, these same people sometimes needed solitude, needed to feel detached, needed to remove themselves from their friends.

As one of my own interviewees remarked, referring to a friend of hers who wanted to see her very often, "I'm quite fond of the lady but I have to recharge my batteries sometime."

Self-actualizers or not, each of us employs ways of creating distance between ourselves and our friends. The techniques we use vary, depending on the person and the circumstance. I have already made the point that we can have gratifying friendships not necessarily based on a great deal of self-revelation, especially of the "secrets-sharing" kind. But it's true that those people who had *some* friend they could use as a confidant seemed the most content with their friendships overall, and that most of us *do* equate self-revelation with closeness of friendship. Of course, self-revelation encompasses many dimensions. It can simply mean, "Here I am, this is me without the mask, this is how I think and feel." It can mean, "I'm going to tell you a lot of private, intimate stuff about me." It can mean, "I've got these personal problems; help me solve them."

I interviewed a number of people who associate intimacy almost wholly with self-revelation, and self-revelation narrowly with problem solving—and who then proceed to distance themselves from others by taking the stance, "I never tell my troubles to anyone," or, "I never cry on anybody's shoulder." That we all do reveal something of our problems somehow, sometime, with someone, if only fleetingly, is quite beside the point. To make it a personal rule never to talk about any personal problem with any friend ("It's none of their business," I was told, and "Why give people ammunition?") is really to say, "This is the barrier I've erected to keep myself from becoming too closely involved with others, this is my way of keeping people at arm's length."

There are many other ways of distancing ourselves. Time is a very common way; we just don't have as much time as we'd like in order to pursue our friendships, we say, conveniently forgetting that we set our own priorities in terms of time. Seclusion is an obvious technique—removing oneself from people until one psychically needs them again. A man I know, a writer, lives in a remote mountain house but every few weeks pops into the city unexpectedly and calls me up or sees me and one or two of his other good friends, takes care of some business, then vanishes again. (Most people who want to isolate themselves do not want to do so completely; even Thoreau, at Walden Pond, recounted, "I had three chairs in my house, one for solitude, two for friendship, three for society.")

"Joking relationships" also do the trick of keeping people together and apart. Some very charming and congenial persons draw people to them—but also ward them off by the simple if unconscious device of cracking jokes, making wisecracks, or hurling mock insults. They are not alone—or unique. Anthropologists have noted joking relationships among some primitive African tribes ("a peculiar combination of friendship and antagonism," one anthropologist, A. R. Radcliffe-Brown, calls the technique); it ameliorates hostility between persons or groups that might otherwise be at each other's throats. Sociologists have noted its use in factories and offices, especially among employees who are at different levels of the pecking order; it's a way of saying, "Let's be friendly but not too friendly." Whenever used by one person or both within the context of a friendship, it means, "I like you and want you to like me, but I don't want to take the risk of getting too close, so my jokes and my insults will define the limits of our relationship."

Collecting people is a paradoxical way of avoiding closeness: the more people one collects, the more friendly one is—but the less chance there is of establishing relationships that involve any significant degree of intimacy. Spreading oneself thin precludes the risk of spreading oneself thick.

Are there then limits to our human potential for closeness? Are we limited in the amount of intimacy we have to "spend"? Folk wisdom has it that we can only give of ourselves to two or three close friends at a time—two or three is the number most often mentioned—and most of my adult respondents agreed. Something about being really close to people, investing ourselves emotionally in them, is very demanding—demanding timewise but, more importantly, demanding in terms of psychic energy. There are a few students of human behavior who suggest that each of us contains a kind of "fund of intimacy" (which presumably varies from person to person)—that we have just so much of ourselves to give, that there are limits beyond which we cannot go because our emotional energy then becomes sapped. "Fund" or not, the more close friends we have, the less close they really tend to become; the more we give to one person, the less we seem to have available for another; the more needs one person fills, the less need we have for others. In fact, when intimacy becomes too intense those of us involved must find ways of drawing back from time to time—or the relationship quickly burns itself out.

"Since my close friendships are more often than not intense relationships, I could not tolerate more close friends than I have," observed a Southern California woman who numbered her dearest friends at four. A divorcee in her thirties, who joined an informal three-hour group discussion on friendship at my home, thoughtfully said, "I don't think I can handle too many close friends. It's too much. Because it's all so heavy when you're so open and so mutually responsible for your friends."

But—folk wisdom again—isn't intimacy supposed to breed intimacy? Being loving further augment our capacity for lovingness? Of course, and there need not be a contradiction. The more "practice" we have in the realm of affection the more warmly we are able to respond to people generally, the more loving we can be generally. But there are still those psychic limits on our energy, especially when we really involve ourselves in a relationship. In fact, it is with the few people we are closest to that our expanding capacity for intimacy shows up most clearly, with them that the relationship becomes ever closer and deeper. Even Maslow's self-actualizer's circle of friends was "rather small," the friends they loved "profoundly" really "few in number."

A final point with regard to friendship and intimacy. The other primary relationships we involve ourselves in—especially the marital and parent-child ones—are, I have already noted, fairly structured; that is, in a host of ways society makes it pretty clear what our moral as well as legal responsibilities are when we become mates and parents. Also, with respect to marriage and family life, "The emotional demands on an individual living in a steady, close, intimate relationship are enormous under the best of circumstances," as Miriam Weisberg of Cleveland's Center for Human Services points out. Though we definitely do expect our friends to meet our emotional needs, our friendships are not clearly defined, not subject to a ready "job description." We don't see our friends as constantly as we see our families, nor do most of us carry on extremely intense friendships—especially not in adult life and most particularly not after we marry. Our friendships give us a special potential, then—the potential for intimacy without the imposition of pressures to be unrelentingly intimate. In effect, our friendships both enhance and offer relief from the other emotional roles we play. As Ms. Weisberg says, "Friendships can help in diluting" the stresses and strains that result from those other emotional roles.

"I love my husband and I adore my children," a housewife in Minnesota told me, "but it's when I sit down for lunch and gossip with a good friend that I feel most relaxed."

LIFE CYCLE

5

Child's Play

FRIENDSHIP is not a "superficial luxury," fine for some children, not so important for others, notes Dr. Willard H. Hartup, director of the University of Minnesota's Institute of Child Development. For all children it is a necessity, vital if they are to take their place in the world of people with some degree of assurance and security.

Of course, no matter how young we are, we already know that. We know it, firstly, by instinct: even very small babies stare fascinatedly at each other. We know it secondly because right at the top of the list of adults we learn to identify, on the heels of close relatives, are family friends; the concept of friendship comes to us early. We know it thirdly because all those concerned adults around us encourage us to know it: few mothers fail to see to it as one of their early duties to coax their little children into playing with other little children, and "doesn't have friends," or "doesn't get along with other children," is a common complaint of parents who seek professional help for their young ones.

Before we can even begin to reach out to other children,

however, we must acquire some insight into the fact that they *are* "other"—that is, persons separate and independent from ourselves. (Some individuals go through their whole lives, of course, not fully convinced that others are truly separate from themselves.) By age two or three or so, it is a lesson sufficiently learned so that we can park ourselves next to an age mate and play (peaceably for the most part) alongside that other child. It is a really significant step on the road to friendship; technically it's known as "parallel play."

By the age of three and a half or four parallel play becomes shared play; very quickly after that we are already becoming comfortable in relating to a group of children. For some children these milestones in their social development occur sooner, for others later. It depends on the individual child—on what that child is, and on what that child has been taught to be. We are born already fixed somewhere though not immutably on that broad scale of sociability that runs from extreme shyness to extreme outgoingness. We are subject, too, to the influences of our home environment; the child being reared in a home marked by a fear or suspicion of strangers, for instance, is hardly as apt to be sociable as easily or quickly as the child growing up in a home in which there is a lot of easy contact with friends.

The friendships of three-year-olds or four-year-olds can already be astonishingly deep and nurturing. In the social science literature there is a remarkable account of six German Jewish youngsters in a British nursery school; they had spent almost all of their lives in a German concentration camp, where their parents had been killed; they had always been together. Their scars showed cruelly: they destroyed furniture and toys; they were hostile or indifferent to the nursery school staff taking care of them; they coldly ignored adults in general. But they were entirely different among themselves—loving, caring for, sharing with each other, showing no sign of jealousy or competition, becoming terribly upset if separated for even a few minutes. The social scientists who observed them noted that, understandably, they were suffering from neurotic symptoms but not from delinquency or psychosis. They had helped each other master their anxieties and develop some social attitudes; they had helped keep each other sane.

The little monkeys made famous by researcher Harry F. Harlow too have shown what a psychic curative even early association with peers can be. Baby monkeys raised with cloth surrogate mothers, brutal mothers, or no mothers at all—but allowed to form affectional relationships with peers—initially showed some social maladjustments but eventually straightened out. Baby monkeys deprived of mothering and of contact with peers for about six months became isolates; years later they still had problems in the area of socialization. "A faithful friend is the medicine of life," as it is written in the Apocrypha.

So already at four our friends become good and effective medicine. It is medicine in the context of play, and—often at that age—role play. The roles we play, and want to play, are the roles that satisfy our needs; they make our lives an open book for those adults observant enough or interested enough to notice. Jimmy and his friends are playing house; Jimmy assigns the "daddy" role to a girl: it says something about him in terms of his sexual identification. Alice always has to boss her friends around: she feels dominated by her parents and uses this means of asserting herself. Freddie is a very competitive boy; he must be bigger, stronger, better than the other boys: though all children are competitive to some degree, Freddie's competitiveness is so intense it is reasonable to assume that someone at home—mother? father? a sibling? —is making him feel smaller, weaker, inferior.

"Children use each other in their idiosyncratic ways," is how Doris Ronald, educational director for the Center for Preventive Psychiatry in White Plains, N.Y., puts it, and this is not all bad. It is, in fact, the way children gain mastery over relationship problems. The specifics of the role do not matter much unless the child always throws himself into the same character—always becomes the passive one, or the powerful one, or whatever—in which case there may be cause for parental concern.

At four we are already pretty good at quarreling with our friends, usually when they don't come through for us in just the way we want them to. At five we have become artful manipulators

—"I'll be your best friend if you'll give me a cookie"—manipulation seeming to be as inevitable as competitiveness in the social repertoire of youngsters. At five or so we are also terrific imitators: we copy with remarkable fidelity some of the traits or mannerisms of the children we have our little crushes on—without being intellectually aware, of course, that we're drawn to these particular friends because they meet our lacks and longings in very specific ways. All this continues, to a greater or lesser extent, through much of elementary school.

And all this makes it understandable that, with perhaps one or two notable exceptions, our preschool and early school friendships are hardly marked by constancy. We are not disloyal to the friends who become ex-friends; we are simply changing, growing, slipping back a bit to a more dependent state, forging ahead some more, testing ourselves against the other children, trying on their personalities for size. Today Ted has a need to lord it over his chums, just as his older brother at home lords it over him. Tomorrow, a month later, a year later, Ted feels surer about himself and no longer needs to be dominant; now the big attraction is a boy more capable of give and take. In between or at some other point Ted may, for some reason, feel especially vulnerable; for that brief time he may be drawn to a stronger boy, one with whom he feels protected. Today Estelle, a moderately extroverted girl, is drawn to an aggressively outgoing young friend; tomorrow some shy little thing has appeal; some other time, chafing over myriad parental and school restrictions, Estelle becomes fast friends with the most rebellious girl around.

I posed a number of questions about friendship to elementary-school students (229 of them) in public schools in three sections of the country—a racially and economically mixed school in Manhattan, a school in the heart of Detroit's black ghetto, a predominantly white middle–upper-middle-class school in Los Angeles—and one of those questions was whether friends should think and act alike. Over two thirds of the children, whose ages ranged from nine to twelve, opted in favor of having some differences between friends. Their answers, especially those from the New York and Los Angeles children, would gladden the hearts of people who see individualism an utterly vanished concept in the United States:

they said that we are not all made the same, that people have a right to be themselves, that it's boring when friends are too much alike. Taking accurate measure of their world, the Detroit ghetto children were immensely practical: it's best that friends don't think or act alike, they said, because otherwise they'll surely get each other into trouble.

Very possibly the children in New York and Los Angeles were more imbued with notions relating to individualism and autonomy, middle-class notions that echo, however faintly, middle-class child-rearing practices. Yet it seems to me that the Detroit children hit upon something even more fundamental. Their overall message appeared to be, "We help protect each other from our destructive impulses"—which in effect is, "We meet each other's needs." That, I think, is the crux of things. As children we are drawn to each other because we share interests and outlooks—but, especially as we grow a bit older, differences draw us, too. Then we enter into relationships that have complementary elements to them because only that way can we use our peer relationships to draw on each other's strengths and shore up each other's weaknesses.

Just as early friendships aren't marked by constancy, so are they not marked by uniformity of need. We need our friends, yes—but we do not necessarily need them consistently. At around seven, eight, or nine particularly, many of us are in and out of friendships—there are times when our world is swarming with friends, times when hardly anyone feels like making contact with us or we do not much feel like reaching out to others. There seems to be a real need for privacy among many of us during this period, a need to spend more time alone, engaged in solitary activities— reading, sketching, watching television, whatever. This really bothers some parents—mothers in particular—who seem to measure their children's attractiveness and good mental health exclusively by the number of friends they have. If the number is not enough from the parents' point of view, they hurry to consult with child psychologists or family-service caseworkers. The chance to be alone, to think, to engage in some "inside talk" is as important for growing children as is the chance for friendships.

There are also parents who worry overmuch because their children have just one or two close friends, never a bunch of kids who call or hang around. Making popularity and only popularity synonymous with good social adjustment and friendship satisfaction, they put on inappropriate pressure to have their boys or girls acquire more friends. But, as Ms. Ronald points out, pressure inappropriate to the child's personality can have only undesirable effects; there are children whose one or two close friends are enough to engender satisfying, growth-promoting relationships. To push such children otherwise is only to court unhappiness: they become angry and insecure, and retreat further, or try to latch on to a crowd and fail miserably.

It certainly doesn't take long, during childhood, for the social rhythms that are ours by choice or circumstance to assert themselves. In every group of elementary-school children there are boys and girls who must be compulsively popular to shore up sagging egos—"people collectors," mini-sized. In every group there are youngsters who, by virtue of temperament or environment or both, feel most comfortable having a good many easy, not-so-intense relationships. In every classroom there are the children who are never crowd joiners. In every classroom, too, there are real isolates, the rejected, the children who simply do not have any friends.

Social psychologist G. Watson perused the relevant literature and concluded that in a typical school class one child out of five is an isolate. It frightens children and brings immeasurable heartache to them to know that they are alone while all the other children around them have their cheerful friendships. In more clinical terms, there is no question among child-development experts that socially inactive or rejected children are, as Dr. Hartup puts it, "relatively high risks for all kinds of developmental difficulties." Inactive or rejected, they offer the same unhappy psychological profile: very anxious, timid about the world, emotionally quite vulnerable, and—often—inappropriately aggressive. Many of them play wretched parts in their family dramas, being crushed by rejecting or overly possessive parents. Such children withdraw, confirming their worthlessness or their inability to take charge of their lives, or become so needful that other children instinctively (and probably cruelly) turn away. There is a widespread belief that highly gifted youngsters are isolates, so caught up by (or pushed into) their talents that they have no taste or ability for social relations. Many studies and observations of gifted children show this not to be universally so at all. Certainly there are isolates among the gifted, but a great many have strong, firm friendships during their childhood years. An intensive study of ten exceptionally creative adolescent girls, for instance, shows that many of them were social leaders as children and in elementary school almost all had at least one or two close friends (though none had a wide circle of acquaintances).

Gifted or not, most of us at seven or eight or nine find it less important to be with the group and more to our liking to spend a lot of time with one special friend, the best friend. Best-friendship brings with it a measure of security for young people who are no longer "younger" children—a "you and I against the world" kind of feeling. At this stage, too, for security reasons we need the exclusivity that best-friendship brings: "That's *my* best friend!"

I asked the children in Manhattan and Detroit and Los Angeles what it is that makes the best friend different from all other friends. I knew they would say that you like your best friend more —which they did—but I was also hoping for more specific distinctions that might indicate something about the way they defined best friendship.

If my sample of boys and girls is any indication, even quite young elementary-school students already know that friendship calls for mutual aid and other forms of reciprocity. "Best friends help you with problems and answers," was a nine-year-old girl's comment, while a boy of the same age observed, "He does nice things for you and you do nice things for him." Most of the boys and girls, regardless of their ages or where they lived, differentiated between best friends and other friends in terms of "more" and "less": with your best friend you play more, share more; you can depend more on your best friend; you like to do more of the same things together. A few children touched on the ideals of friendship proposed by the classic writers on the subject: "A good friend encourages you to do better," wrote a perceptive twelve-year-old Los Angeles girl; a twelve-year-old in Detroit, equally sensitive, said that a best friend "understands you better than your other friends."

Thus, early, do we build up our images and expectations with regard to close friendship. Everywhere the boys and girls were remarkably in agreement with each other and with their counterparts elsewhere (some of the older Detroit children excepted; they were unique in emphasizing the money, favors, and help that friends can give you—again reflecting the facts of ghetto life). Everywhere they were saying, about best friends, "Here's someone you can trust, someone who accepts you and affirms your worth and lovability, someone with whom to share pleasures, someone to go to in times of trouble."

No disappointments or disillusionments? No inkling yet among children of nine or ten or eleven or twelve that in the real world friends can let you down as well as boost you up? They know; we know. When they responded to a question about what is the worst thing that a friend can do, the children in New York, Los Angeles, and Detroit gave many answers, but they all amounted to the same thing, and it can be summed up in two words: rejection and betrayal. The worst acts of friends? To hurt you, fight you, cheat you, turn on you, the children said; to exclude you when some other child comes along; to lie about you, snitch on you, blab a secret, stop being your friend. Acts of hypocrisy were often mentioned as cruel acts in friendship: "Talk about you behind your back," said a sixth-grader in Detroit; "Play a dirty trick on you," said a fifth grader in New York; "Pretend she likes you but doesn't really," responded a Los Angeles sixth-grader.

Throughout the fun times and angry times and blah times and disillusioning times during these childhood and preteen years friendship is our means, our society's means, of helping us master our feelings and deal with our environment. Friends are second only to parents in helping us grow into "socialized" human beings; in fact, some of the functions friends perform cannot be performed, or performed too well, by parents.

First of all, childhood friends do the most fundamental job of all: they help us to begin the process of helping us to separate ourselves from our parents; childhood friends are the first link in the chain of "others" that leads from our families of origin to whatever families we ultimately want to create or belong to on our own.

As we pursue our relationships with them, friends teach us how to be aggressive in acceptable ways, how to cope with the consequences of our aggressive acts, and how to handle the aggressions of others. (Timid boys and most girls do not confront aggression—rough-and-tumble play, fights, and the like—so directly as children; hence, as adults, they are at a disadvantage in functioning altogether effectively in an aggressive world.)

Through friends, early in life we become introduced to the world of sex; even the most sensitive, straightforward of parents cannot be as effective sex educators as they might like to be; so pervasive is the incest taboo that children frequently tune out, or "forget" what their folks tell them about sex.

By virtue of how they relate to and accept us, friends help us to become more secure in our sexual identity. Along with parents they help us to define what society calls "masculine" and "feminine," and—in some of the more sophisticated young social circles today —help us to break out of the rigidities that mark traditional sex roles.

Friends as well as parents and other adults reinforce the workings of our consciences, and in other ways contribute to our moral development. Sharing is a case in point: studies by Hartup and others show that in childhood generous peers are important resources in developing our capacity to respond generously and altruistically. If we are the sociable kind, then one of our good friends is the important good influence; if we have few social contacts we tend to be more impressed by, and model ourselves after, children who are comparative strangers. But model ourselves we do. So these are some of the ways we use the first dozen years of life to prepare for the next sixty; these are some of the ways we use our friends to help us accept ourselves, live in the world with others, and love.

6

Joys and Agonies:
Teenage Friendships

WE are teenagers and friendships are a joy. We are teenagers and friendships are a despair. We are teenagers and our friendship experiences now, like all our other experiences and reactions now, are unique in their intensity.

That sounds so sweeping a generalization, as though all adolescents are run off the same emotional assembly line, complete with interchangeable psychic parts. Far from true. Within the context of our shared experiences—growing up, growing away from home (though a part of us still longs to remain a dependent child), grappling with all the physical and emotional changes we are going through—our responses as teenagers are still idiosyncratic. We certainly do not conduct our friendships all in the same way. Some of us go through our adolescence without any, or with hardly any, friends; some of us have loads of them; some of us make friends we will treasure the rest of our lives; some of us play it cool ("So they're friends, big deal"); and some of us need friends less than others because of certain life circumstances in which we find ourselves.

The only child needs friends more than does the teenager with siblings close in age living at home. Twins need friends less than nontwins. A Japanese team studied hundreds of twins, both identical and fraternal, and concluded that their friendships are not so intimate as the friendships of nontwins are. Those of us who feel our parents do not understand us need friends more than those of us who feel our family relationships are fairly comfortable ones.

But we and our teenage friends can give each other something no one else can: because no one else, no one but our age mates, is going through what we are going through—those confusing, mysterious contradictory impulses that are constantly darting about inside ourselves. In some respects the teenagers who talked to me about their friendships differed among themselves; that depended on who they were as persons and at what stage of the teenage cycle they found themselves. But among them all, despite geographical and age differences, there was remarkable uniformity in what they wanted and valued in friendships. Their views were of course much clearer and more definite than those of younger children; there was a much sharper tie between personal needs and attitudes toward friendship.

Trust and its offshoots—loyalty, honesty in the relationship, discretion—are very important to almost all teenagers; it was the first thing usually mentioned, understandably so in that the teenage years are those in which it is most difficult to trust ourselves and our mercurial emotions. From trust flows acceptance: "I trust you to accept me as I am." Feeling so peculiar, so unlike what we were, to be seen and accepted as we are may be the greatest gift our friends can give us at this time. "What's important is to have a friend who understands your feelings—and doesn't criticize" is the way a ninth-grader, a Minneapolis girl, put it.

Having things in common is important. Hardly any teenager I interviewed opted for the mirror-image approach, but almost everyone talked about friends having similarities in certain specific ways. Naturally we want to be like our peers, like a lot or like a few of them, at this stage when we think of ourselves as so different, in a negative sense, from everyone else. With a number of the younger teenagers interviewed, sharing activities, enjoyably doing the same things, was right near the top of the list. At this stage we are not so concerned about ideas, not so ready to tussle with them; friends' divergent views tend to puzzle or disturb us. With many of the older teenagers "shared values" came up again and again as a must in friendship: "Even if you don't have that much in common—one likes sports, the other doesn't—if you share the same values then knowing that person, relating, makes him a friend," said an eleventh-grader, a student at the Bronx High School of Science in New York City. Several of his classmates nodded agreement. Expectedly so: when we are crystallizing and integrating our values, what a marvelous feeling to discover and be with others who feel as we do in such basic ways!

Throughout these years our hormones are working overtime, a phenomenon we have in common with our friends and a phenomenon we share with them. In our culture, at least, our teenage friends are as vital to our sexual success, then and later, as they were important in earlier years. We help each other sexually. We feed each other sexual data—share fantasies, talk about what we would like to do sexually; this is gossip in the service of recreation and procreation. We compare penis size, breast size, and the like; compare with each other our developing physical selves so as to have the answer to a question that plagues us at twelve or thirteen and nags us afterward: "How do I stack up physically against others of my kind? Am I too big? Too small? *Am I okay?*"

We share our fears and our thirst for information, via gossip, tales, jokes, and lurid passages in paperback books. We joke a lot about sex, jokes being a comfortable way for us to deal with a subject we are not even in the 1970s altogether comfortable in dealing with directly. And because we gain reassurance from each other and because we feel close to each other in experiencing these scary, exciting bodily changes of ours, and because we aren't yet ready to reach out to opposite-sex friends, we reach out to each other. Some of us do so tentatively, others of us very directly. Homosexual play—played out broadly or narrowly—not only is common in early adolescence; some form of it seems to be an inevitable happening even on the road to heterosexuality. Putting it another way, as psychotherapist Oscar Rabinowitz points out, before a boy can have a girl friend he has got to have a boy friend;

before a girl can have a boy friend she has got to have a girl friend. Time passes and most of us tend to forget such episodes, or see them in a different light; some of the biggest locker-room jocks turn out to become some of the biggest homosexual-baiters later on in life. And of course some of us respond to our emerging sexuality by denial: trying to smother it by the sheer weight of intellectualism; we confine ourselves to the world of books and ideas, find friends who do likewise and, in our fashion and for the time being, feel relatively safe.

As teenagers we belong to an exclusive club not of our making but of circumstance. The peer group being as important as it is to us, peer-group influence is tremendous. This obviously varies: boys and girls who underneath it all have very strong wishes to remain dependent often fight this by becoming fiercely devoted members of the peer group, much more so than those who feel more secure about growing older and assuming more responsibilities. At any rate, few of the teenagers I spoke with were intensely devoted to the generation gap, at least to the extent of another Bronx High School of Science student, a male student who said, "As far as my life is concerned with respect to my parents, I lead kind of, like, two different lives. My parents don't really know about 99 per cent of me. If they did, I could never live with them. Things are different with my friends because they actually live the bulk of my life with me." Most were much, much less cut off from their parents. They are influenced by their friends and they go to their friends for help and comfort—at least the majority of those who admit going to anyone do—but they go to their parents, too. Parents have a rather heavy influence on school grades and on their adolescents' educational and occupational vistas. Many youths told me, too, that they talk to their friends about problems with parents—and to their parents about problems with friends.

But many boys and girls also had violent, passionate reactions to something their parents do in connection with some of their friendships. And what is that? To try to drive a wedge between themselves and a particular friend. To try to break up the friendship. The youths believe their parents have their best interests at heart but are nevertheless being utterly misguided. None hinted at the other two possibilities: that their parents are expressing concern based on a realistic appraisal of the situation, perhaps with respect to sex or drugs, the two most explosive issues—or that their parents, prompted by their own particular fears and anxieties, or haunted by memories of their own wild adolescence, overreact.

No denying this: as teenagers we bleed, we agonize, when our mothers or fathers tear down a friend of ours. When it happens we are torn (though we might never admit it, even to ourselves) between loyalty to friend and loyalty to parent; we are afraid the criticisms may be justified (in which event we would have to deal with them); we cannot escape the fact that when our close friends are criticized it is also we who are criticized. The whole issue leads to great anger—"I hate 'em when they do that!" spat out a young man in California; it leads to ugly scenes. "I don't want you to see Ann any more, she's a streetwalker," a girl in Winston-Salem reported her mother as having told her, and she reported her own reply: "Look at yourself, Mother." In the end, parents have little influence on their teenagers' friendships.

Whether boys or girls we're equally vehement about parental interference, but in some other respects we differ, male and female, in the way we look at and engage in our friendships. Beginning a pattern that generally carries through to and throughout adult life, boys base their friendships more on doing things together, girls more on the sharing of emotions and reactions to experiences. For girls more than for boys, sharing activities is a vehicle for sharing emotions. Girls tend to be much more emotional about their friends, too. Early on, at twelve or so, many girls already have some pretty specific romantic-sexual fantasies about boys, and trade these with their girl friends—while boys still fantasize about being great football players, scientists or doctors. Though boys are aware of girls in a specifically sexual sense, it is still the latter fantasies that they trade more with their same-sex friends. The results of a study of over four hundred Southern teenagers suggests that girls more intensively than boys—and earlier, too—use peers as their most important "reference group."

Why such differences? Girls have a harder time separating from home (cutting themselves off from their mothers); they mature faster and go through more striking physical changes than do boys; girls are freer than boys to express feelings, lean on friends, show affection. Many, many boys are still bugged by the fear that to be close to a male friend is something akin to homosexuality. In part this is changing; boys are more open about their feelings than they used to be. A high school senior in Boston told me, "You talk with a guy about what you're going to do later on in life, about your fear of making decisions, and you've been thinking, 'Wow, I'm the only fool in the world who feels that way,' and all of a sudden you find there's somebody else who feels that way." He said this quite without embarrassment in front of a group of other boys and girls, and some other boys too were as open. But the stereotypes of traditional masculinity are still powerful indeed.

Competitiveness is another element of significance in boy-girl differences. Of course, we are all, practically from infancy on, competitive. Psychiatrist Edward Sheridan of Georgetown University divides preadult competition into three distinct and fascinating parts, each concerned with mastery: *The first five years:* The struggle to master the wish to remain a baby—which children instinctively understand, since the easiest way one child can wound another is to yell, "You baby, run home to Mama!" *The second five years:* The struggle to master brain power—learning English, math, whatever, doing well in school—not being called "retard," or "dumb" or "stupid" by the other kids. *The third five years:* The struggle to master the biological and social changes that then take place—and the worst insult then is to be called "queer" or "different."

In adolescence we are all intensely concerned with our bodies— what is happening to it? how does it look? how well do I use it?— but the way this is expressed often differs between boys and girls, which is at least in part a "tribute" to the cultural impositions that do so much to shape us. For boys the concern shows up more around speed or muscles or other achievement. For girls it is more (overtly, at least) a matter of looks, dress, popularity and, when dating begins, who gets the dates.

Both boys and girls have best friends—and do not have them. Many of the teenagers I interviewed talked with warmth and insight about their best friends—and about the meaning of the best friend; many others, though, disclaimed the existence of best-friendship in their lives: we, they said, hang out in groups.

Best-friendship is supposed to happen in adolescence—supposed to in the development sense—because of need: in turmoil, this is our rock; in a sea of change, this is our anchor. The best friend is truly the one we feel safe to be very sad or happy with, the one who gives us solace in times of heartbreak such as parents divorcing or a death in the family, the one who supports us emotionally and who, like an externalized conscience, cautions us at times—a brother by choice, a sister by choice. A girl in Los Angeles said, "With a best friend you don't have to spell everything out"; a boy in New York said, "Your best friend knows you better than you know yourself."

But there is also the teenage group, gang, clique. Belonging to a group gives us a feeling of status, of power, of "us against the world." The group is also a refuge: reduces the risk of committing oneself to, and being disappointed by, someone. So powerful is the teenage group that some of us belong without really wanting to—or feel guilty for not belonging. A college student in Los Angeles wrote, "Maybe there is something wrong with me, but I think that I am actually unable to make friends in groups. . . . When I get out of a one-to-one relationship I start feeling closed in. I hope there are others around like me who also dislike group relationships. . . ."

The ambivalence about best-friendship came out most strongly in my interviews with California teenagers, maybe because group life and therefore group pressure is probably strongest there. When I brought up the subject of best friends to a classful of eighth-graders in a junior high school near the Los Angeles International Airport, few acknowledged having such friends. But as they spoke up and became animated, something else emerged. A girl: "You 'sort of' have a best friend." Another girl: "You have lots of friends but you don't want to concentrate too much on one person." A boy: "If you have a couple of friends and you call one your best friend, what does that make the other—just okay?" A girl: "If you have a best friend I guess you're lucky—but most people don't say 'I have a best friend' to each other."

Yet things are not always as they seem. If we say, "I don't

want to single out one friend over another," we may be saying any number of things at this point in our lives about our ability to be assertive (nonconformistic), about our willingness to commit ourselves to a specific relationship, about the way we were raised (never to play favorites). If we say, "Best friends may be fine for some kids, but I don't need it," we may also be saying that we consider the relationship kid stuff, sissy stuff—after all, aren't we supposed to be able to stand on our own two feet now? If we say, "My allegiance is only to the group," we may be saying, "I'm afraid, too afraid, of homosexual involvement to risk having a close same-sex relationship."

In fact, there are teenagers who prefer to spread themselves a bit thin in group friendships, but there are many other group-oriented teenagers who nevertheless, upon closer questioning, agree that they have warmer, more trusting relationships with one or two of the other members of their gang. And there are teenagers who already do what most adults do: they go, as a Bronx Science student said, "to different friends for different things." They have several good friends who, together, form a kind of composite best friend.

During adolescence some of us—for whatever time we need—form fiercely intense friendships with one special person, making the world a place almost exclusively populated by the two of us. We consult each other on everything, tell each other everything. Many teenagers idealize their friends and try in certain respects to be like them, but if our tie is very intense we carry this to an extreme: two bodies with but one ego. Why? Because at this point in our time we may be feeling desperately vulnerable and dependent, may need to give each other this kind of desperate parenting. We have found each other, a miracle; we cannot risk more. Sometimes one friend may *seem* like the "stronger" of the two, the one who does more of the parenting—but if both have need to shut out the larger world, both are equally vulnerable underneath.

Hopefully we do not need to cling forever; what happens then to the clinging relationship? It can go either way. We discover ourselves in different ways, and that is the crux of the matter; we change. Referring to a friend with whom she has been most open, a sensitive sixteen-year-old in Winston-Salem, North Carolina, told me, "For a long time I tried to be her, I admired her so. That was wrong. I have to be me." Another girl in the same group, a year or so older, said, "My best friend and I—we used to be very much alike, do everything together, the whole bit. Now we aren't so alike as before, and we don't share the same experiences as we used to. But, you know, we're better friends now than we ever were."

So it can go well; it does if the two friends change similarly and there is an underlying respect between them. But often it does not happen so fortunately. And then? Then the one friend's "I have to be me"—meaning the *new* me—clashes with the other friend's plaint, "Where is the old you?" and the friendship, no longer held together by the glue of meshing needs, ruptures. We say, "What did I ever see in that person?" (We mean, "How could I ever have been drawn to that type—and what does it say about me?") There may be an abrupt clash (unconsciously precipitated by one of the friends so as not to prolong a painful situation) or a slow fading. Either way, it is the end, sometimes with hard feelings, sometimes with none. Like the law of the jungle, the laws governing teenage friendships can be harsh. But then, paradoxes are characteristic of the tie we call friendship.

Generally speaking, not only speaking of very intense bonds, the course of teenage friendship does not run smoothly. Bickering, jealousies, hurt feelings, misunderstandings, and the feeling of "How could you do this?" or "How could you do this to *me*?" expressed in one way or another is all part of the adolescent scene. There are two strong and contradictory forces in us just now; they serve to create tension in our friendships: egocentricity still there from childhood, only more finely honed—and there is idealism. We idealize our friends but when they do not fully serve our needs we have a strong feeling of having been let down. And because during our childhood and adolescence our emotions are so much more on the surface than they are later on, so much less controlled, we do not much attempt to rationalize or excuse, as we are apt to do later on. Instead, we are outraged. We love and we hate, but mostly we forgive and are quick to love (or like) again.

When teenagers talk to me about the ways in which their friends have hurt them, all those painful hurts coalesce to form one overall theme—assaults against the person: being put down by a friend, being insulted, being ignored or left out or not paid attention to when our friend becomes friends with another (the classic triangle situation superimposed on same-sex teen friendships, a very common complaint, especially among girls—at least they verbalize it much more), and having something we told our friend in confidence blabbed all over town. That really hurts, that we share something private about ourselves and it becomes common property: our friend has made *us* common property.

The more intense the friendship, the more anguish such acts produce; the more intense the relationship, the sharper the love-hate pattern (in childhood as well as adolescence) emerges. Then too, the very intensity produces its own resentments: we may need to be so dependent on another, but we need not like it. When we are troubled we may get the friends we should have (if we're lucky) but not necessarily those we want. I recall junior high school with sadness still; it was, for me, a troubled time. I wanted to be friends with the "in" kids, wanted their popularity to rub off on me. Instead, I became close friends with a shy, insecure boy who wasn't good at sports but was good at sitting on the sidelines—a boy like me. It would have been damned lonely without him, yet I resented him as he must have resented me. In each other's company, we were reminded of ourselves.

Most troubled of all are the teenagers who have no friends at all. For some of the more sensitive boys and girls there is a noticeable ebb and flow to their outgoingness—there are times, they may be protracted times, when they need to withdraw to find themselves. To find their independent selves. But all of the experts I spoke with agreed that really prolonged isolation marks a deeply unhappy kid.

Boys and girls can be friends without, in the narrow sense, being "boy friend" and "girl friend"; at least more are becoming so. Dating is something else again. Our friends make important contributions to our psychosexual development; then, when those of us who do so "discover" the opposite sex it can easily upset the balance that our friendships have had. The start of dating—a word out of favor in the teenage lexicon just now—can go either of two ways. Two good friends can do a lot of sharing around this scary and exciting time—can share feelings, fantasies, fears, and experiences. But if one is more popular than the other it can also provoke envy and resentment, stifled or in the form of little digs. Once one of two friends becomes serious about somebody else, abruptly much less time is given to the old friendship; then the left-out friend thinks or says in some fashion or other, "How come you're never around any more; don't I count, too?" or, "How come you're so close-mouthed now, when we used to tell each other everything about our dates, lay it all out in the open?" Girls leave the shelter of the peer group earlier than boys in search of girl-boy relationships; in addition to their sexual-romantic notions, Dr. Sheridan observes, girls are far readier to dream of having genuine friendships with boys than boys dream of having them with girls. How competitive we are during this early dating time, both boys and girls, showing off, proud to have our sexuality—or at least our sexual identity—confirmed.

During adolescence, even late adolescence, we are hardly the epitome of social maturity, and it really does require a good deal of tact to handle the conflicting demands of the new romance, which is so compelling, and our old friends, who want us back. But some teenagers are more tactful than others, making efforts to be with their friends or drawing their friends into some of their activities. Group dating, so popular now among teenagers and probably born as a way of avoiding too-serious sexual confrontations, is a big help. Of course, some teenage friendships flounder and break up on the shoals of the new-found heterosexual scene.

Teenage friendships break up anyway, and by no means only those that have been very intense. Unless we have all grown up in the same small town or constricted neighborhood, and all remain there, we do not as adults so readily retain more than one or two friends from our adolescent days. And as we pass through those days, our progress is marked by the corpses of dead friendships. Some we mourn—did we not expect this bond to last forever?—while some others, so solid once, become as insubstantial as soft ice cream in the noonday sun, and as little lamented. When our need is over we depart; it is that cruel fact of teenage life.

Turning points in our lives have a radical effect on friendship bonds throughout our teenage years. There is the shift from elementary school to junior high: "When people go to junior high they feel more mature and their little childhood friends they met in kindergarten or whatever, they decide that—well, I've had this friend for a long time but I think it's time I went out and got some new friends because I've kind of outgrown them," said one of the eighth-graders in Los Angeles, a sharp, articulate girl. Sounds blunt, cold; she did not use jargon—"Your needs no longer dovetail." But it is what she meant. (Junior high school, by the way, can be a boon to boys and girls who did not do well socially in grade school: more kids to choose from and no self-contained classrooms to lock you in with the same bunch of kids every day.)

Then there is the shift from junior high to high school: suddenly, such differences—inside, outside; differences in being, looking, acting; in the space of a few weeks, it almost seems, we have become other persons. "Someone you were best friends with in the eighth grade turned completely different over the course of a summer," said a high school sophomore wonderingly, not stopping to think that her friend might have had the same reaction about her. Casual friends are the first casualty, but sometimes it is also the erstwhile casual friends who now become the close ones.

Because so much of our lives center around school throughout these years, it is oftentimes hard for a friendship to survive when each of us goes to a different school, and this is so even if we live in the same neighborhood. The neighborhood, after all, is not where things are happening. If one friend leaves for a parochial school, or departs from a parochial school, the cleavage becomes even sharper. Our classmates, teachers, experiences are so different that we no longer have a common reference point for gossip. As one girl put it, "I think the best kind of friend is someone who can understand you without your having to say anything—and when you're operating in two different atmospheres you lose that."

Throughout these years we keep on picking up bits and pieces of learning about people, through learning about friends, and consequently we learn more about ourselves as well. Steve, in Los Angeles, told me that now, at fourteen, he no longer opens his mouth to say the first thing that comes to mind when he hears a friend say something he vehemently disagrees with—he knows it hurts feelings, and he doesn't want to alienate friends. Several of his classmates agreed that, as one grows older, one becomes more careful with friends. (There was no time to pursue the theme to its logical end: when does tact end and dull conformity—marked by stifled feelings—begin?) In Boston, Alice, a year younger than Steve, told me that when she was in elementary school she had a couple of close friends and they did everything together; now, Alice said, she cares more about other people and wants to have friends everywhere.

Jim, in New York, a sophomore in high school, told me that he feels closer to his friends now than he ever did—but that they test each other more now, too. Mary, in San Francisco, talked about finding it easier to accept things she dislikes in friends now, things that would have gotten in the way before. Ted, a high schooler in the same city, talked about no longer seeing some guys he had hung around with because they were on hard drugs. Taki, a sophomore at Georgetown University, told me that in junior high she was just with a bunch of kids; in high school she picked her friends more carefully, became more selective.

There is order in the chaos, and chaos in the order, of teenage friendships. We want to hang out with the gang, but we want to be close to somebody too. We want to be close to somebody, but we don't want to shut anybody out, either. We want to trust fully, but discover that people let you down—while at the same time we are ready to drop the friendship if our needs aren't being met. We start with shared activities and end up looking at the whole person. We want our friends to help us grow, and find we have to protect ourselves from friends who might put our own vulnerabilities too much to the test.

What shall we call all this? Life? Growing up?

7

The Singles Experience

NICK is twenty, Greek, a student at Georgetown University. His family came to the United States right after the Second World War, determined to hold on to and nurture a cherished Old World tradition—that of a strong family life. "This is not so true of me and of other Greeks my age," he told me as we talked in the hushed quiet of a darkly paneled meeting room on campus. "We have the same problems and the same desire for advice and support as other young people have." He paused to reflect a moment, then said, "But it's changing. I used to love my friends—it's changing. Tradition has affected me. My brother now has two children for whom I have deep affection and it's almost like filling a parental role. I feel all the attachment that went out to my friends before, in high school, has now centered in more closely on my family. Though I still get something from my friends—they open up to me new areas of my character."

Dominick, nineteen, Italian-American, lives in an Italian section of Boston. He works in a foundry. As a teenager he hung around with a gang that had two things in common—a love of mischief and a dislike of school. He hung around with a gang, he hung around in a poolroom; his was a tough, male-oriented world that constantly reaffirmed traditional masculine values. While a senior in high school he met the girl he is going to marry, the girl he loves and who, in his eyes, will be the perfect mother for his children. His foundry job came soon after meeting her, and the gang is nothing but fond memories.

"But two of the guys I grew up with, we're still pretty tight. We play poker every Wednesday night and I figure that's never going to change. We go in and out of each other's houses like family," Dominick told me.

Cindy is twenty-three, "an embodiment of WASP culture," as she put it, fresh out of Bryn Mawr, working in a Manhattan publishing house. Hers is the life of chic singles bars and flamboyant Fire Island summers. While in high school she was one of a tight-knit bunch of girls; they exchanged secret signals and cheered each other up when things became weepy. In college, she found, she no longer needed that kind of security and formed a very close friendship with one girl.

"It was fantastic how we clicked—music, dancing, boys, the art scene," she recalled, "we did it all together. But then college ended and she did a straight trip—married an insurance executive, moved to the suburbs, joined the Ladies' Aid Society or something, the whole bit. I didn't dig that at all. I was bridesmaid at her wedding, but afterward it wasn't the same. We'd get together every once in a while, but it was like we were growing farther and farther apart. Now? Now we exchange Christmas cards."

"Singles" is a term so broad as to defy meaning: eighteen-year-olds clutching their brand-new high school diplomas and weathered ninety-three-year-old widowers are singles and so is everyone unmarried who fits in between. Even "young singles" is too loose a term; as Nick, Dominick, and Cindy show, we are too diverse a group still.

High school is no great melting pot. We tend mostly to stick to "our kind" in terms of race and social class, though having similar skills and interests, and pooling our resources (as in sports and theater arts) does push some holes through those barriers. Beyond high school there is a big shaking out: we no longer share the common school experience, and while we are still teenagers and shaky about our identities, we are no longer teenagers in the younger, more intense way.

Going to college or getting a job will separate us. Going to college locally or elsewhere will separate us. The friends we retain will be mostly those who grow as we grow, or to whom we are tied by bonds that go beyond the ordinary. "When did you meet your longest-standing friend," I asked nearly sixty of my respondents, "and what is it that keeps this friendship alive when so many others presumably have fallen by the wayside?" Most of them by far said that junior or senior high school was where they had first met their oldest friends, those years where we go through some pretty intense moments together. And what is it specifically that keeps these friendships going? A few distinct patterns highlighted my respondents' replies: the friends most apt to be our lifelong friends are those with whom we have shared experiences we consider important, and who change as we change, at least to the extent that our values and "styles" do not become too discordant. Even if we move to opposite ends of the country and only see each other but once or twice a year, the feeling of the old friendship will remain.

"Young singles" friendships aren't as intense as in adolescence, which is not to say they lack significance. They are very significant both despite of and because of our tasks during this stage of the life cycle: getting more schooling and/or getting a job, pursuing active sex lives, developing romances and maybe getting married. We are expanding in terms of ourselves and our lives, and it is scary to expand alone; we are experimenting with the things life has to offer, and it is scary to experiment alone; our characters are still forming and it is through friends that we see better who we are and how we stack up against other people. Mirror, mirror on the wall: that mirror in our rooms is not the most accurate of them all; we need to match our self-perceptions against a hard-nosed reality—the way others see us. The process never ends, but is most crucial in the younger years.

First, the college experience. Friends are easier made in small colleges; groupies are more the thing in large colleges in order to reduce society to a more manageable scale. But some who have been to both kinds claim that relationships in small colleges tend to be shallow, while in the large ones even being comfortably ensconced in a group does not make the feeling of anonymity go away altogether. Fraternities promote close friendships—and it is interesting to see that fraternities are enjoying a renaissance. College commuters are at a serious disadvantage in forming friendships, especially when, as often happens, they are shy persons in a big place. Commuters who involve themselves in activities that engender a sense of community—campus politics, the school paper, drama, or the school band—are much less at a disadvantage.

That friendships are superficial on campus is a complaint I heard from students in all types of colleges. "We become close for a year and then we don't see each other that much," is the way a biology major at Connecticut State College put it. "There are some first- and second-year students I'd want to become friends with, but it takes all my ingenuity to get together with them once or twice a year—our paths don't cross, or if they do cross, we're going in the opposite direction," is the way a young Harvard professor put it.

Every school from nursery school on is a self-contained social system of sorts, encompassing cliques, groups, and networks; the higher the level, the more complicated the system. Just as the Azande in Africa need friends in order to navigate safely within the parameters of their world, just as we in the larger society use friends to help fill us in on the myriad details we need to know in order to carry on our daily lives with some degree of efficiency and coherence, so do college students need other college students in order to function well in their milieu.

Our college peers (and especially peers who are friends, whom we trust more) help us in a variety of ways we take for granted but would sorely miss if we were surrounded only by uncommunicative strangers. We study together—and it seems we do a better job of studying when in the company of persons we like: researchers at the West Virginia Institute of Technology have turned up evidence to show that college roommates who are computer-matched for compatibility earn higher grades than do students who are randomly paired. With college friends we can mutually bitch about rotten instructors and poorly designed exams; in other words, we can give each other sympathy and support. Having college friends enables us to measure ourselves better against others: we can compare notes with them about how much studying we are doing and how much extracurricular life we are sacrificing; this is one way, too, in which norms are set on campus. With friends we discuss what courses to avoid, how much studying to do, what the professors' expectations are apt to be, how much we can get away with, generally how to be selective in our college work. With friends we exchange notes and views and gossip on what the finals are going to contain, and offer each other reassurance after the exams are over.

But we are not only in college to grow intellectually and creatively; hopefully, we are also struggling to better realize our creative potential. College friends can help each other enormously in that regard—people who respect each other thrashing out values, reaching inside themselves and each other to crystallize attitudes, watching each other and learning from each other and helping each other on heady flights of introspection. "The thing that is remarkable and sometimes difficult for me is that in some places she has 'mellowed out' and I haven't," reported a young student at the University of Wisconsin, referring to herself and her very close friend. "This is usually a question of self-confidence. I am every day closer to a real hold on my own confidence but sometimes I get scared. My friend and I often get all excited and confident (it's like living magic; the energy of feeling you're a 'good person' is so vital) but then I'll know—feel—realize—accept that I'm not there yet. She kind of draws the goodness out of me that I don't yet quite believe is there. She is helping me by doing that."

College can be a very lonely place without friendships that are cemented by so much trust, but not only college. To the extent that such things can be measured, we are lonelier in early adulthood than in later adulthood, before marriage than after marriage, after retirement than before retirement. The loneliness factor is a reason "singles" is not only a catchword now but an industry—a multi-million dollar industry encompassing singles bars, discothéques, coffee houses, resorts, apartment complexes, and other such manifestations of our need to meet. We go to or live in such places for sex and/or romance and/or to be confirmed as desirable, but not only. We also go as a response to loneliness.

Loneliness is not a simple void that friendship inevitably fills. Sometimes a friend can help enormously; sometimes a friend can —well, just help. No friend can replace a beloved mate or lover who died. No friend can fill the emptiness felt by the person who hungers for a mate or lover but has none. But the companionship, warmth, and perhaps affection that the friend offers make the loneliness easier to bear, and certainly alleviates less intense feelings of isolation. Most of us who go to singles bars or dances do not go alone. A law student at the University of Arizona, now a social worker, was candid about why he and the guys in his fraternity house went places together: "We'd never admit it but it was our way of sharing anxieties; we had a common situation and common problems." A young woman in Tustin, way south of Los Angeles, California, spoke about her sorority and about her subsequent relationship with roommates out of college: "We need our roommates—for more than sharing the rent. If we don't have dates it's our roomies we go to night spots and dances with. We don't want to be alone in a new situation, we want the strength of another person."

At the Club Continental, a singles apartment house hard by Disneyland, residents did not say they were there for companionship—except, of course, opposite-sex companionship. And most of the young residents I talked with agreed that the friendships they have made there—where the apartment turnover is very high—are casual; they have close friends, but their close friends live elsewhere.

Yet that is by no means the whole story. As one observes the young men and women on a Saturday afternoon, casually emerging from their apartments to join others for talk, card games, television watching in the recreation room (open twenty-four hours) or at poolside, it is very evident that there is some sense of community here.

For many Club Continental residents this is a way station of sorts: the first time they have lived away from the parental home, or their first residence upon separating from spouses. Not uncommonly, two residents with bachelor apartments strike up a friendship and decide to team up for one of the more spacious two-bedroom apartments. A number of loners are attracted to the place: they are shy, have little to do with the other residents, stay in their rooms a lot—but are in some way nourished by being in the midst of others of their age group, rather than holing up in an anonymous apartment in an ordinary, anonymous neighborhood. It is as far as they can go in reaching out—and far better than nothing.

In and out of singles compounds, a fact of life for many of us in the single state is roommates. And they are not an unmixed blessing. We may need them—we do need them—but we must also live with them. In other situations friends offer us the choice of being with them or not, accepting their foibles or removing ourselves when those foibles become too stressful for a time. Living with a friend removes the freedom to come and go that characterizes other friendship arrangements; it shifts the perspective and puts fresh burdens on the participants.

John and Ted in Austin, Texas, are an example: they were very close, they thought they saw eye to eye on most things; then they become roommates, and a thousand minor things, like not cleaning up the dirty dishes, conspired to make them odd couple out: "After a while it has to do with feelings," mused John afterward. "If your friend is so unconcerned about your feelings you finally take it as an insult."

A roommate friend can quiet pangs of loneliness; a roommate friend can also make one feel more lonely. For instance, despite all the lovely stories about the beautiful-dumb girl who rooms with her plain-brainy friend, each somehow making up for the other's lacks, such stories do not usually end so nicely, not if the plain one sits alone in the apartment every Saturday night. The beautiful one winds up feeling guilty, the other resentful.

If both are reasonably attractive and popular, competitiveness has a knack of stealing in. Lisa, a researcher in her thirties, told me her story: four years rooming with the same friend, each caring about the other, helping when sick, being intellectually stimulated by the other . . . the constancy between these two roommate friends was unusual, dazzling. And there was a reason for it. They were different kinds of personalities, one more reserved and intellectual, the other more the bright and bubbly kind—and they attracted different kinds of men. But then Lisa, the quiet one, changed as the city stimulated her; she acquired more verve, became more outgoing—and found herself attracted to, and attracting, her roommate's type of men. A happy situation became unhappy; Lisa moved out; now the two women are friends again, but living apart.

Lisa, and several other single women too, said they found less competition among a group of women friends than in a one-to-one friendship. In the group "there are beautiful but unstated rules of the game—if you have dated or are clearly interested in a man the other girls stay away." It's always the same with a group: as long as its members need it, they quite naturally evolve the rules that ensure its survival.

Singles need friends, but friends are not stationary items, like toys to be played with when the mood is upon us. One day we look and the toy is not there. There is a constant and consistent pressure on single people in the larger cities, particularly, to change, to meet new people, to form new relationships—the eventual price for not doing so being isolation. The reason? Our friends keep getting married, or finding somebody to live with, or leaving the city, or otherwise changing their status.

"There's a constant turnover," Marge, a beautician in Manhattan, explained. "I've gone through several periods in which I've almost had too much to do—so many friends, lunches, evening things to do. Then I've had periods where almost everybody has left to get married or something, and there is a certain feeling almost of having been deserted. Your married friends don't stop being your friends, but it isn't the same, either, because they aren't available like before. Being single you have to keep making new friends because if you don't you'll soon find yourself all alone." It is a pressure that can become exhausting.

People go, people come. Being young and single and fairly new in the big city and working in a tension-filled office where there are a lot of other newly arrived singles, where do we form our first friendships? In that office, among those other singles, of course. The need for support and companionship is very strong; the relationships we then form tend to be very close; the demands we make on each other are very intense. But this intensity has little chance of lasting, because the circumstances that engendered it do not last. We start getting used to the city, becoming acclimatized, meeting other people, dating, finding better jobs in other offices— developing new networks of relationships . . . And a year or two or three after it was born, that close group of friends is close no longer. In fact, we hardly ever see each other and when we do things aren't the way they used to be; contact is a little strained; eventually we stop seeing each other altogether.

How could we have been so close and now not even want to be together? How cold-blooded are we? Well, things are not so simple, so brutal. We are not now what we were then; our need for that kind of closeness, belonging to an especially vulnerable period of our lives, is no more; maybe that need was the main thing drawing us all together and we didn't have that much else in common. And maybe, too, some underlying feelings help create the distance: maybe when our need is too great we don't respect ourselves as much, nor the friends who have the same need, and don't want to be reminded of it when that period of our lives has passed.

During our teenage years we discovered sex and romance, but for a while, in early adolescence, dates were almost like a counterpoint to the really intense friendship tie. Later on in adolescence boy-girl contacts became an end in themselves, yet were not apt to conflict too much with friendships, especially if a lot of our dates really consisted of group dates. After high school things change. At first group dating is still popular; quite a few younger college youths told me dating really consisted of a bunch of kids getting together. But after a time "a bunch of kids" is too much of a crowd, then double-dating is the thing: because it's cheaper to go in one car, because it's fun to be with friends as well as dates, because it's still nice to have some moral support, especially if the date is fairly new.

Sooner or later, though, all the world is not a stage upon which we feel comfortable performing; we prefer a more intimate setting upon which to develop and play out our romantic interludes. Other people become a distraction. Friends become a distraction. We need our friends; at least we need to know that they are there, and to replenish the supply, so to speak, when they depart—but it is fair to say of most of us that our eyes and ears are turned to love in any or all of its dimensions.

What do we want? Mates? Lovers? Romances? One-night stands? Whatever the motivations that prompt us to date, an ever-present element is the pressure to be authenticated as attractive, desirable, masculine, or feminine. We are not rewarded by our peer group nor given to patting ourselves on the back for our talents as good friends. Money talks and sex appeal (a readily marketable commodity) confirms.

To what extent we need that confirmation depends upon our sense of equilibrium—that is to say, our sense of personal security. Society may propose, may influence—but we dispose. And there is room, after all, for both friends and lovers. But if we yearn mightily for a "relationship," if we are prone to be "addicted" to one person—well, then we are apt to devalue our friends, at least until things go wrong. "One of my friends is living with a man," a young artist told me, "and she has cut off all her friends because her whole attention is now devoted to him. She'll only see us when he's busy or away." Sadly, the artist added, "We're all hurt by this—we're second-best now." If we have a strong need for reassurance we might not cut our friends off as abruptly as all that, but we will date like mad, and as for friends—well, there is so little time for friends.

Maybe these patterns are at an extreme, but then again maybe not so very. A great many singles, in describing their "working friendships" vis-à-vis dating experiences, gave virtually identical accounts—ones that amounted to friends taking the position of "second-best." Say Helen and Suzy make a date to go to the movies on Friday night. About the middle of the week John, an attractive bachelor, calls Helen to ask her out for that same Friday night. Helen unhesitatingly accepts, then calls Suzy to cancel, explaining the reason, knowing her friend will "understand." And Suzy will, because in her life too dates take precedence over friends. (I deliberately used women in the example because many more women than men described this pattern as occurring in their friendships.) But however much the friends understand—and they truly do, knowing the important meanings a date has—they are still confirmed as counting not as much.

Yet in another way our friends count for a great deal. They serve a very specific and intimate function throughout this period, especially when a casual date becomes something rather more serious in our lives: we bring those new boy friends or girl friends around, show them off to our friends, wanting to share our joy, wanting to wax a little triumphant, too—but also wanting them to approve of this person we have come to cherish more, in a sense wanting them to act *in loco parentis.* A number of singles, both heterosexual and homosexual, spoke of this. In fact it was a gay art director, approaching middle age, who summed it up most feelingly. "In the last ten years I must have had a hundred boy friends," he said, "and all my friends, straight and gay, were always going 'ugh!' Then I met Jimmy, and they all liked him—still do. It makes me feel so proud, so content."

When our friends like our lovers it is reassuring ("if they like him they must think he's good for me"). And it creates a warm, companionable feeling all around: my community has accepted a new member. And it confirms to us again that we're okay ("if they think he's nice, and I chose him, then I must be nice, too"). ·

As the love relationship follows its natural progression, either to abort or to culminate in marriage or a marriagelike arrangement, we do not see our friends very much. Nevertheless, we use them—use the more intimate ones—a lot during this sensitive period: we look to these friends to give us encouragement and other kinds of support, to commiserate with us when upsets occur, to share our happiness when the course of true love runs smoothly, to be a sounding board for the echo of our feelings. And more subtly, without necessarily identifying the emotion, we take comfort from the fact that our friends are "there," even if in the background of our lives, for to be in love is to be exposed and our friends serve as invisible but very real security blankets.

8

How Marriage Affects Friendships—and How Friendships Affect Marriage

IDEALLY marriage results in the merger of two families—his and hers; we know it does not often work out that smoothly. Ideally marriage results in the merger of two "families" of friends; we know that this too does not often happen. Describing the effect of marriage on his premarriage friendships, a young Haitian school paraprofessional sighed, "It's a difference like night and day." And then he recounted for me the story of old friends, close friends, who are close to him no longer now that he has been married for a year.

Things do not necessarily work out so drastically for all of us, but there is no doubt that the nuptials begin a sorting-out process that will eventually leave us with very few of the friends we had in our single days. This is not the way we plan it. We do not cold-bloodedly say, "Well, my life and my needs are different now; I don't have any more use for my old friends." Yet something of the sort does happen—not right away, but in time. More immediately there occurs a different kind of sorting out: she may have tolerated (pretended even to herself to like?) his friends before the marriage, now becomes more critical of them. They may have had their negative thoughts about her, too, but held their peace. After the wedding such goodwill loses some if its force, tensions come more to the fore; everybody knows, even if no one articulates it, that there are going to be redefinitions on all sides.

There are, of course, also certain practicalities that contribute to that redefinition. We are no longer free to come and go as we please. We do not have the time to do the things we were accustomed to doing—going to the movies, having a few drinks, or going away for weekends with friends. We may use the practicality of time—or lack of it—to help structure us in our new situation: to say we don't have the time to see old friends when in truth we do have the time and the inclination but feel our new mates will mind; or to tell them we have no time when in truth we do but simply want to be with our new mates; or to tell them that time is a problem when the problem really is the fact that we no longer want to see them.

So I am forced now to think about Stanley, with whom, during my first year in New York City, I went to whatever parties we managed to be invited to and whatever of those Friday-night paid dances (this was before the advent of the singles bars) we thought might be most appetizing. Stanley was a jewelry designer and I was a writer. I'm not sure we had that much in common, philosophically or intellectually, but some powerful similarities drew us together. We were both decent, modest guys feeling the pressure of a tough, unfeeling Manhattan world. We were both lonely, of course. We both wanted to find girls, not only to sleep with but to hold-hands-walking-down-the-street with, and to kiss gently on a summer day's ferry ride to the Statue of Liberty, and perhaps to marry. Well, the time came for me; I met the young woman, I married. Stanley was genuinely happy for me. But though I don't recall that we ever discussed such feelings, my departure from our dumpy single state must have made him feel all the more lonely; on some level he must have been a little envious and therefore resented me a little. Or at least resented a fate that had, at that point anyway, smiled more kindly upon me than upon him. I know I would have been happy for—but resentful of—him.

Well, Stanley designed a beautiful, and beautifully unique, wedding ring in the form of a double-knot, Chinese style, for my half-Chinese bride-to-be and I swore (to myself if not to him) that we would often have him over. He came once. He came twice. He might have come to our place three times, and we had lunch together on occasion. That was it.

My wife was acceptant of Stanley, and Stanley of my wife; that was not the problem. (Though it does strike me now that she did not find him as stimulating as she did some of my other friends.) It may be that he no longer wanted to see me: I had lucked in; those Friday night dances were no longer for me. But that's pure speculation; again, we never talked about it. I do know that I suddenly, rapidly, lost interest in seeing him. Just him. I retained other premarriage friends and even now, fifteen years later, they are friends still. No, my reluctance to continue the friendship with Stanley had to do with circumstances other than the fact that he was still single and I was not. Perhaps all we had in common, after all, was the blahs—we were comrades in loneliness. Perhaps I didn't want to be reminded of that—of my feelings about myself as we went about our clumsy way trying to alleviate our condition. There is no other way to say it but to say it bluntly: I had needed Stanley, I no longer needed Stanley; he became a memory and, thinking about it now, I am sad that it had to be so—but, it seems, it had to be so.

I have dwelt at length on Stanley and myself simply to suggest that, in addition to the obvious forces prompting a redefinition of friends made prior to marriage, we are also subject to a host of feelings, some fairly subtle, that determine which friends remain and which become memories. Redefinition, however, does not by any means always result in a fading away of the friendship. Some of our close friends remain close, some remain but on a more casual basis, and some casual friends become closer (often the married ones, if our mates get along, too).

Yet in the best of circumstances things change; the way in which the friendships are played out, and the place they have in our lives, change. Our focus, as marrieds, is the marriage, the family. The ordinary course of married life does—unless the two partners are, or become accustomed to, going separate ways—create a shift: "I swore it wouldn't happen, but it did—I fitted my friends into my marriage," is the way a young woman aptly put it.

The main thrusts of our psychic energies generally are directed toward the marriage, children, possibly relatives, and the job or career (though not necessarily in that order). If in our single state close friends at some point tend to become "second best" because of the fervor of our courtships, once we are married they occupy secure but well-defined places in our lives—assuming of course that they are important in our lives to begin with. They can no longer be measured in ways that make sense of "second best." We are not discarding or ignoring them. We say, in effect, "You are dear to me but yours is a supportive rather than primary role in my life. Your presence helps me to function better as mate, parent, worker, citizen, and links me more securely to the outside world. All this is very important. But there are priorities."

It is not a thought-out process. If the marital relationship is a reasonably good one, then as a natural consequence of that fact we do tend to be most open, most relaxed and intimate, with our spouses. Intimacy with friends remains significant, but the edge is taken off it.

This also creates more or less obvious alterations in the way we relate to friends, especially close ones. For instance: many people who once were very candid in discussing their sexual lives with friends now tend to pull back somewhat, to be more restrained because they are talking about their spouses as well as about themselves, and presumably behind their spouses' back. With feelings of love or affection come feelings of protectiveness. The friend who is left behind understands. Well, understands intellectually. Often, nevertheless, the changes do bring on some feeling of being excluded.

That inevitably friends don't have as high a priority as does the family in most marriages should not obscure the really vital role friends play in relation to the marriage itself. Without good friends my mate and I would live in a world that for the most part (give or take some relatives, if they happen to live nearby) is populated by the two of us. It follows then that we must count on each other, my wife and I, for everything—for laughs, for a shoulder to lean on, for a handkerchief to cry into, for the give and take of intellectual exchange, for any and all of the emotional needs we may have at any given moment. We make of each other the sole repositories of emotions. This creates a tremendous burden on each of us to be everything to the other. We are left, as agency workers at the Catholic Service League (Akron, Ohio) put it, without the "coping mechanism" by which we can "drain off" feelings of anger and frustration we cannot confront our partners with. We are left without outlets to dilute the intensity of our relationship. We are leaving ourselves open to isolation should anything happen to the marriage or the marital partner; people who put everything into their marriages and nothing into their friendships are often left feeling quite desolate when something suddenly happens to alter their well-ordered married life.

Marriage counselors are the first to point out that marriage cannot meet all our needs. In point of fact, there seems to be a significant correlation between a couple's well-being and the extent to which they lead an active, integrated social life. When the aerospace industry was at its most active, aerospace families, highly mobile, often failed to establish friendships in their communities, turned inward, became increasingly dependent on their families—and bred growing hostility that often resulted in divorce. Large-scale family-socializing studies show that the more we, as couples, have in common with other couples who are our friends, the less likely we are to get divorced.

I encountered a few couples where both partners agreed that they sufficed unto each other and did not need friends. Much more often, where friendlessness prevailed, it was one of the partners who had no friends, relied completely on his mate, and in effect said, "My spouse is everything to me, my best friend, my only friend, the one I always turn to." And in almost every instance of this kind the partner on the receiving end of this overwhelming dependency (much more often the wife than the husband) would indeed feel overwhelmed. Would say to me, either directly or in a roundabout way, "I wish he'd find a friend!" These things are never simple; it may well be that at some earlier stage the nurturing spouse invited all that dependency from her mate but only later on, with the changes that life brings, feels oppressed by it.

Such couples are in a minority. Most of us, as marrieds, have friends. Our marriage styles tend to dictate our friendship patterns. We do not begin married life, usually, with many married friends, or with many friends who from the outset "belong" both to ourselves and to our spouses. The longer we are married, though, and the more we see ourselves and our mates operating as a unit, the more married friends we tend to make and to relate to on a couple-to-couple basis. Conversely, the less "togetherness" we practice in our marital relationships, the less apt we are to have many couple-to-couple friendships. If the marriage is characterized by devotion but also by fairly heavy individual involvements in the outside world, both patterns are apt to be strong ones. Among my married respondents, 27 per cent said they saw most of their friends separately, 31 per cent reported couple-to-couple as the major pattern, and the remaining 42 per cent claimed both patterns to be important ones in their lives.

Social class plays a role in this. Sociological studies undertaken over the past couple of decades or so generally show working-class families much more than middle-class families to be characterized by rigid definitions of the roles that men and women play, by little emotional sharing, and by separate friendships. Also, working-class families (especially wives) have been shown to be more kin- than friend-oriented; while middle-class husbands, far more than middle-class wives, are said to initiate family friendships. But I found these traditional patterns to be changing: as egalitarian pressures exert some influence on working-class male-female relationships, there is more sharing of friends among them. As workers become more mobile, leaving kin behind, they become more friend-oriented; of fourteen workers I interviewed in an electric plant in Winston-Salem, North Carolina, for instance, 40 per cent said they visit more with friends than with relatives. As middle-class wives take more active and responsible roles at work, in voluntary organizations and elsewhere, they also become more active in initiating couple-to-couple friendships.

The dynamics of couple-to-couple friendships are clearly more complicated than those engendered on a one-to-one basis. The way it usually happens is that two people come into contact as the result of a shared interest or activity, become friendly, then say, "Why don't we get together with our spouses?" At this point things become much more tricky. For instance, my wife introduces a new friend and that friend's husband. If a family-type friendship is going to develop (as contrasted with periodic but more casual encounters) the other husband and I have to get along. My wife's friend has to like me and I have to like her. My wife has to like her new friend's husband. It certainly helps if the children get along too and if there is some rapport between all the adults and all the children; child-child or adult-child antipathies can be rough on an incipient family friendship.

The odds that we are all going to click are not that great, so a lot of incipient couple-to-couple friendships fall by the wayside. But many of them work very well, which is remarkable when one considers all the people who have to match up. Of course, there are things going for such potential friendships, too. First of all, we generally have a predisposition to like the people our mates bring in, and it is a pretty well established fact of friendship life that if you think you are apt to like someone a reinforcement process is at work nudging you toward actually liking the real person. Then, too, we are generally attracted to people rather like ourselves, so we are apt to have something in common with their mates as well. And the four people do not necessarily have to like each other equally well. Often, in fact, things are not that symmetrical and not everyone is liked equally well by everyone else. Such couple-to-couple friendships can be good ones, as long as everyone remains flexible and tolerant. But they are not likely to develop into the ultimate of couple-to-couple friendships—the integration of two families into a larger family unit, at least in a psychic sense, marked by affection, concern, intimacy, and a considerable sharing of lives.

Friends are helpful in reducing marital tension, but friends are sometimes a source of conflict in the marriage. At times conflicted couples become very busy socializing with friends, keeping active with other people as a way of avoiding each other, avoiding coming to grips with the issues that divide them. At times friends are a poor influence, disruptive to the marriage. More often, perhaps, friends are used as a weapon by one partner or both in an ongoing battle whose dimensions far exceed the surface issues being battled about. Like money, sex, and children, friends can be used by one partner or both to goad, wound, retaliate for other hurts, or otherwise destructively. "Joe thinks you're wrong, too," says a husband to his wife, referring to his best friend. "You're no good just like the bums you hang around with," says a wife to her husband. With remarks like these, friends are used like a club by one spouse to beat down the other.

I contacted two dozen family-service agencies—agencies that counsel troubled couples—to find out just how friendship is a conflict issue among couples with marital problems. Though these agencies represented a geographical cross section, they responded as though with one voice. Predictably, the major issues family-service workers presented were friends interfering with the marriage, friends being seen by the spouse as bad influences ("He runs around with a crowd that gambles," "Her best friend is a divorcee who likes to go to bars"), friends taking sides with one partner against the other—and friends as an isolating influence.

By far the major pattern alluded to—by over two thirds of the contributing agencies—had to do with friendship being an isolating force in the marriage. One mate spends a lot of time with friends; the other mate feels excluded.

This is no simple issue: how much time out is too much time out? As with every other facet of human interaction much has to do with motivations: why is the one spouse spending so much time away from home, if indeed it is so much time? Why is the other spouse objecting? More specifically: a young factory worker marries, then hangs around with his bachelor friends evenings and weekends as he did before marrying, and this makes his wife unhappy. Is he saying he's not yet ready to accept the restrictions of married life? Is she saying she's afraid he'll be tempted to return to his bachelor life, so best he stay away? A suburban matron's evenings are taken up with club meetings, ceramics classes, the opera (which her husband hates), and other such activities; her husband objects vociferously. Is she saying she finds more satisfaction in her outside activities than she does in the marriage? Is he saying a wife's place is at home and she has no right to go out? A construction man goes fishing and hunting with his buddies when the season is on, and his wife is sick and tired of staying home alone weekends. Is he being thoughtless—and hostile—in leaving her alone? Is she seeing in his behavior confirmation of her fear that she's dull, not much fun to be with? A man very handy with his hands spends a lot of time fixing things at a friend's house but never at home, which his wife deeply resents. Is his behavior a reflection of underlying anger at her? Is she being possessive?

There is no way to answer such questions, of course, without probing into the family dynamics that occur in each particular case. Often there is no single answer because both partners are involved; destructive marital and family patterns generally gain life from a kind of collusion that occurs between all those involved.

Strangely, the family agencies did not touch on a problem I encountered a number of times while talking to husbands or wives about their friendships. But then, not so strangely, because it is something most people tend to resign themselves to rather than bring to the attention of counselors. Nevertheless, it causes frustration, even pain. It is the problem of one spouse being outgoing and sociable, the other spouse being reclusive. The reclusive persons sometimes—by no means always—also turn out to be the dependent ones, content to be nurtured (but needing to be nurtured) in the bosom of their families.

The conflicting needs of gregariousness and solitude aren't so easy to resolve. Compromises are not often very workable; the more reclusive partner usually doesn't have the flexibility required to work out a genuine compromise satisfactory to both; keeping distant from people is the only satisfactory outcome for that partner. The more flexible spouse has choices: to make friendships separately, to give in and live a life of very curtailed social activity, or a combination of both. Usually it works out to be a combination of both. A wife comes to mind: she is very active politically and in her children's school; her husband "needs a tremendous amount of privacy," as she put it, and has no close friends. Only once in the ten years of their marriage have they been close to another couple. The wife said, "Once it dawned on me—gee, it's been three months since the two of us talked to a third person together outside of our own kids." A husband comes to mind: he is a fairly successful scientist; his wife, who does not work, is content to live a quiet life without the hustle and bustle of people coming in and out of it. Whenever he wants to invite people from his laboratory, his wife demurs; they should be invited to those people's houses first, she says. He knows social life makes her uncomfortable and does not push it, but it severely restricts his friendships. He said, "I know I can't have them over, so I've been keeping myself more distant from people than I might otherwise be. My need for friends is strong, probably stronger than during some earlier periods in my life, but I do less about it now. My expectations have diminished. A kind of numbing goes on over time."

Friends, directly or indirectly, may be a source of conflict; friends may also be drawn into an ongoing conflict simply because they *are* friends—because we trust them and feel we can go to them when we are troubled. Not everyone goes, however. About half the married men and women I talked with still retain a deep sense of privacy, if not about all matters then about family affairs, even in these days when self-revelation is seen as the ultimate good in encounter groups and on television talk shows. Some saw it as a betrayal of the marriage to talk about family problems. At times people would mention close friends suddenly divorcing without themselves having had any inkling of it beforehand. One woman related how she and a bunch of her friends had gotten together a few days earlier and talked about the little time their husbands, all career-oriented men, devoted to their children—"and you know," she added, "it occurred to me afterward that none of us, who were the mothers, really came out with how *we* felt about this."

Yet it is hard to see how seeking the advice of trusted friends, or merely using them as a sounding board, is either a betrayal or a gift of friendship. The crux of the matter is what we, caught in the maelstrom of conflict, feel most comfortable doing. Crucial, too, is why we are doing it. To share fears, anxieties, uncertainties, and other difficult feelings pertaining to the marriage with a trusted friend can be rewarding experience: it can make us feel less burdened, less isolated, and provide us with a fresh perspective. Besides, if we are used to being frank and revealing with a particular friend, to keep wholly mum about this subject would be in the way of setting up an artificial barrier: "I trust you about everything but this." On the other hand, if we wish to unburden ourselves only to "tell on the partner," or to gain an ally, or—in the case of sex problems—to titillate, then that is surely a betrayal.

Conversely, when we are on the receiving end of a revelation we have our responsibilities, too: to offer a sympathetic ear, to be as objective as we can; not to take sides just because the talker is "our" friend; to sort out our own emotions before we react and above all before we give advice (overreaction almost surely breeds poor advice); to suggest a disinterested third party, a professional, if the situation warrants it; and not to take advantage in any way of the facts we have been told.

As happens during other stages of our life cycle, during marriage we gain friends, developmental changes occur, circumstances alter, we lose friends. Several couples, for a long time childless, told me virtually the same story: while unsuccessfully trying to have children they became very good friends with other couples in a similar situation, but the moment they did become parents those other couples dropped them flat. Is the pain and envy of seeing others get what we want too great? Is there—absurdly, but is there—some sense of having been betrayed ("We were all in the same boat and now you let us down")? Was only the heartache of not being able to conceive, plus some superficial fun, all that those relationships really amounted to?

Children can be instrumental in bringing adults together in friendship—in the neighborhood, at school meetings, around the playground. Several city mothers also related almost identical experiences: while sitting on benches in the neighborhood playground, watching their little ones play in the sandbox or pedal away on their three-wheelers, they start to talk to other semibored mothers, talk again, a relationship springs up as they see and speak to each other day after day, eventually they even get their husbands together.

Thus two-family friendships are born. But the relationship, warm and close though it may be, does not last forever. It is still the mothers—their motherly concerns, their frustrations—that are the key to the overall friendship of the two families, and the commonalities that drew them together in the first place do not last forever. One moves (even a move a few blocks away, near a different playground, alters things), one gets divorced, one starts working and hires a babysitter to bring the child to the playground, the children reach school age and split up, going to different schools. . . . Certain kinds of reinforcements are no longer present and the playground friendship generally fades after it is five or six or seven years old.

Directly or indirectly, children can break friendships, too. The fundamental reason is values: we don't need to share values on everything, but our ideas on child rearing and our friends' must be fairly congruous or too much tension is generated for the friendship to work. A number of people told me how potentially beautiful friendships soured either at the outset or along the way because of friction (overt or covert) about children and discipline. "Once you have children they don't stay out of the conversation very long," several women said, implying that if shared viewpoints were too divergent talk becomes unpleasant. More concretely, friendships break up mainly because a child is felt to be a bad influence or because a child is allowed to "run wild." Referring to one of her neighbors, a mother in a Manhattan apartment house said, "In her place anything goes, the kids can write on the walls, break things, you name it. She's a sweet, intelligent woman, our two children are almost exactly the same ages, and otherwise we could be friends. But I can't inflict my child-rearing views on her and I sure don't want my child exposed to her approach."

Divorce and the death of a spouse can have a profound effect on friendships. The bitterness that so often accompanies divorce creates a pervasive oversensitivity that easily corrodes the relationship between friends. Betty and Allan broke up amid great emotional turmoil. We visited with Betty, we visited with Allan. Allan, by far the angrier of the two though he had been the one to walk out of the marriage, said, "You saw Betty—you're on her side!" We weren't on either of their sides, we'd hoped to be friends with both. But anger, guilt, a mixture of painful feelings, prevented Allan from understanding that. We saw each other once or twice again, but things were clearly stiff and strained; we lost contact. No, more accurately, Allan chose to break it and I did little but acquiesce.

Even when there is less anger divorce precipitates upheavals in the friendship network. Especially so when friends are either "his" or "hers" and then become "theirs." A split often results in a reordering of allegiances—"theirs" becomes "his" or "hers" again. A recent divorcee, therefore a divorcee recently hurt, told me, "When we get married our best friends feel shut out; they no longer feel they have an intimate place in our lives, and they drop away. We make new friends, lots of them because their husbands are friendly with our husbands, but when we divorce they drop away. I think it's really too much to expect that a couple that was friendly with you and your husband, and brought in by your husband, will be friendly with you alone." But the reaction of the divorced party may also produce negative vibrations. Another thoughtful divorcee told me, "They [friends from the marriage] were reluctant to continue the relationship, and that hurt. But in fairness I wasn't all that eager, either. There were some I was suspicious of—I figured anything I said would get back to my husband. With others, well, they reminded me of a situation I didn't want to think about too much—my marriage." She did keep, she said, friends she'd made for herself before marrying and those she'd gained on her own while married.

Both divorced and widowed persons—particularly women—talked about feeling that some of their married friends no longer responded to them in the old way: now they were single, available, a threat. At a Parents Without Partners get-together for widows and widowers in New York City, a number of women spoke up about this. "Your friends look at you differently and maybe so do their husbands—so to keep peace in the family you give it up," a widow in her forties remarked, with mumbled assent following from some of the other women.

There is also an unalterable reality: when we and our spouses relate as a unit to other couples, and then we are no longer part of a unit, we no longer necessarily share the same concerns and interests, and our styles of life certainly stop dovetailing the way they used to. Persons suddenly single again want to pick up the threads of their lives, work out new modes for themselves, probably look to meet new companions, lovers, or mates. Money is often a problem; that means they can't reciprocate dinner invitations or go out with friends as they used to. Possibly the divorced and widowed persons in such situations themselves have ambivalent feelings about being with people whose lives they shared in happier times. And so they too may not try as hard to continue the contact.

"They invited me to dinner about once a month or so at first," a widower at the Parents Without Partners meeting told me, referring to some married friends and their reaction after his wife had died. "But gradually the invitations came less and less frequently; now I don't see them but once a year, if that." He didn't take it personally, he said, that was the way things worked out. He didn't seem to mind.

Many of the circumstances that force us to reevaluate and make changes in our relationships are readily identifiable. We may not be able to pin down all of our feelings or the feelings of the friends involved, but we can certainly point to precipitating factors like getting married, getting divorced, becoming widowed. Other circumstances may not be so readily identifiable or apparent, but they affect our attitudes toward friendship, our friendship patterns, and the way we relate to individual friends. When we were younger the strongly supportive, advice-giving aspects of our friendships played a much more intense role for most of us than they do now. These are still an important facet of many friendships but aren't as readily drawn upon as before—not only because we may have understanding spouses now to use as sounding boards but also because presumably we are more mature and therefore more autonomous. Our dependency needs never end (much as some people pretend they do), but they do lessen with the passage of time and the growth of self. So as we approach middle age, if not before, we tend to relate to friends more on the basis of shared interests, on developing certain aspects of ourselves, and less on helping each other structure our lives.

Work makes a difference in friendships. The years to and through middle age are the most productive ones in terms of work, but work takes energy. The process of building or maintaining a business or career takes energy, psychic as well as physical. This means less time for seeing one's outside friends or for forming new friendships. But such narrowing is deceptive. Many if not most jobs bring us in contact with people, give us a chance to socialize a bit or a lot, and takes the edge off our appetite for contact. People in working-class or lower-level business jobs usually make a strict separation between work and home—it really was a rare blue-collar interviewee, for instance, who said he saw his work friends on the outside—but it was also a rare blue-collar interviewee for whom work friends were not important. With many professional and managerial persons there is no such strict division between work and nonwork: they do not live a nine-to-five workday and there is a great overlapping of friends. Especially among professional people, the colleagues one works with are the colleagues one plays with. Business and professional lunches and meetings, so often called a waste of time, may or may not accomplish their stated goals, but do provide the opportunity for socializing—which is one good reason why, despite all the complaints heard about them, they are still very much a convention.

Growing older is a factor that affects friendships—that can, in fact, profoundly affect them. Many persons in their middle years told me, "It's harder to make friends as one grows older." They meant, usually, that one becomes more rigid, more settled in one's ways, as one grows older. That may be so for some people but there is an alternative explanation and it has to do with having less of a need for a wide gamut of friends, knowing better what one wants, being more selective, not being willing to settle for less.

Dr. Daniel Levinson of Yale University along with several colleagues had been conducting a searching five-year study of the psychosocial development of men, and some of his research fits in right here. Men (Dr. Levinson's study group was entirely composed of men, which is not to say that women are necessarily very different in this) go through something called the "mid-life transition." This is more than just a melancholy sense of being "over the hill" at forty or so. Though a recognition of one's mortality and an awareness of bodily decline are significant features, it is a developmental milestone because throughout this period men are forced to undergo something akin to an adolescent identity crisis. Now it is no longer a question of "Who am I? Where am I going?" Now it is more a question of "What am I in relation to what I wanted to be?"

Dr. Levinson stresses that whether or not a man is materially successful is not the issue. Somebody can be very successful financially, or make a respected name for himself in some field, or otherwise reach a sought-for goal, yet find his success empty. The issue is whether the "inner" person with a poignant if hidden vision of self and the "outer" worldly person conform, whether the outer reality measures up to the inner dream.

The mid-life transition is seemingly inevitable, but some people also undergo a severe crisis at this point—it is when they make heroic attempts to match their life stuctuies with their inner selves. Tremendous upheavals can result. For instance, there are men who give up their high-paid executive positions to become innkeepers in Maine or return to college for doctorates in fields of social relevance, and/or throw over proper wives for hippie girl friends, and/or conclude that their adult relationships overall, including friendships, are shallow and meaningless, and find other ways of departing radically from accustomed lives.

To be frank, I encountered very few men—or women—who had drastically altered their entire styles of life. A striking example is a very successful businessman who was in a near-fatal automobile accident; the shock of nearly dying and the prolonged hospitalization he was forced to undergo gave him plenty of time to think, to realize that for all his worldly success the person he wanted to be did not in the least mirror the person he was. He ended up devoting most of his time to the establishment of a home for disturbed children, and all his new friendship associations now stem from that activity.

I did meet a significant minority of men and women—most in their fourth, fifth, and sixth decades of life—who had or were going through some kind of reevaluation insofar as friends was concerned. This is not to say that most had sat down with themselves, as it were, and formally conducted a self-interrogatory that culminated in a shift of friendship patterns. Often it was only after we talked for a while that it dawned on them how much of a change had taken place. The process was a gradual one, and often an unconscious one.

Consciously or unconsciously, the realization sets in that time is short and life is precious, that touching and being touched by other human beings is powerfully enriching, and that such contacts are not to be taken for granted. There follows the corollary realization that too many of one's relationships do not come anywhere near fitting the definition of enrichment, and that time is much too valuable for such a thing to continue. Then is when, consciously or unconsciously, a weeding out of friendships occurs —nothing dramatic, just a slow process of letting go of some friends and making more of an effort to cultivate or be with others. An administrator in San Jose, California, said, "I don't any more want to spend my time with people or in places where I am frustrated, I want to spend my time with people or in places where I get pleasure, where I can share, where I can be intimate." A production manager in New York, who noted her own efforts to eliminate friendships she was continuing to carry on simply out of ennui, said, "It's stripping down to the core—making my time count with people who count." In North Carolina a plant manager, after musing about his friends for a while, said, "You know, I haven't seen Mike and Ted for nearly a year. They call once in a while but I haven't really felt like making the effort, I guess. But Bill and I—Bill is a guy I really respect—have been getting together a lot, or just talking on the phone about things. We've become very good friends." He puzzled about that for a moment; then, with a slight shake of his head and a bemused smile, he said, "You know, I didn't realize it was happening."

9

Golden Years,
Golden Friendships?

WHAT are euphemistically called the "golden years" can truly be a golden time for us in terms of friendship. We have the leisure now as we have not since childhood to be with our friends and to enjoy their companionship. We enjoy them for more than companionship, however. The children are out of the nest; there is an emotional void, and friends can do a lot to help fill that void. Retired from work, we no longer have the opportunity to kibbitz and socialize with our work friends—when we do, we find we don't have that much to say to each other any more—so other friends can help fill that void, too. (As the work ethic makes less of an impact on American society in general, a growing number of us are discovering that retirement can be *fun*—at least when we do not have to eke out an existence with tiny pensions and inadequate Social Security payments.) If we are used to being separated from our spouses during the workday, but suddenly are in each other's presence twenty-four hours a day, it can require a big adjustment; spending time with friends helps relieve the pressure, gives us chances to occupy ourselves outside the home.

Most of us in our older years want our children rather than our friends to help us in the big and little ways we may need help—maybe as a confirmation of love, of caring on their part, and maybe also because we think it is "right" since we took care of them for so many years when they were young. But children are not always around, or even willing to be so helpful when they are, or maybe we think it is better to act as independently as we can in order to keep on good terms with them; in such cases friends are of inestimable value in a practical sense and in the sense of feeling "I'm not alone." If our hearts ache because we think our children neglect us, it can be a great relief to discuss this with a sympathetic friend, maybe a friend who also feels neglected by his or her own children. Then, too, there is something about being with a group of friends that keeps us more active, more vital, more "alive" in the richest meaning of the word. This is borne out in a fascinating study by sociologist Zena S. Blau with people over seventy years old: those belonging to friendship cliques were far more apt to consider themselves "middle-aged" rather than old than those who were not members of a clique. A man pushing sixty-five told me, "You know, when I see my friends looking young I feel as young as they look. I don't fear aging so much."

Another study points up the importance of having someone to unburden ourselves to in later years: older people with confidants are better able to cope with the death of a spouse, more apt to have good morale and be a lower risk in terms of mental health, than older people without confidants.

When we are in our late sixties and beyond, we are "typed"—and the typing is usually on the unpleasant side: we are all bored, all passive, all dependent, all at odds with our situation in life, all lonely, not all but many of us tending to isolation. The truth is rather more complicated, for we are a far more diverse group of people than we have been given credit for. Surely some of us—many of us?—are bored, passive, crotchety, dependent. So are a lot of younger people. But there are enough older people, people in their seventies and eighties, who are marvelously vital, alert, interested in people and things, who never stop learning or growing, seeking or questing—and who have very rewarding friendships with persons much younger than they as well as with persons their own age.

A gentleman from Illinois, in his seventies, wrote me a glowing note about how he and his wife still travel and through her efforts —"the friend-maker in the family"—make friends in every community they stay in for any length of time. A vigorous lady of the same age told me how she gets on the phone and talks for hours to her dear friends every evening after eight—when she has put her senile husband to bed. A study of over 1500 working-class men and women in Philadelphia showed that the proportion of isolates among those sixty-five and older was only eight percentage points higher than of those fifty-four and younger.

The physical and mental toll of our accumulated years affect us differently, some of us much less than many others. Our differing personalities also play their part in determining how we will react in older age, of course. We are what we are: we bring to the senior era of our lives the temperaments we were born with and the persons we have learned to be; we also bring our attitudes toward friendship and the way we have grown accustomed to using friends and behaving with them. As in earlier years, how we handle our friendships is revealing of our personalities as a whole —and often, in old age, of our attitudes toward aging. A man in his late sixties, for instance, assured me quite vehemently that he does not have any friends over forty-five—after that, he said, "they get to be old and fuddy-duddy"; he didn't realize the anger he felt toward his own aging and how much he was denying the process. A German-Jewish man and wife told me how alone they felt; all their friends were dead or had moved away. When I inquired about the possibility of meeting new people at a nearby Jewish center, they looked horrified; later, their daughter told me how they had always avoided people "beneath" them intellectually. As we grow older our rigidities become more rigid, our anxieties more acute, our passivity—if that has been our tendency —more pronounced.

Many older persons told me they find it harder to make friends: takes too much time, too much energy; "It's not worth the effort," more than one person told me. It takes effort, of course—but *more* effort if we are not used to making too much of an effort anyway, if we haven't learned the skills, or if we have become habituated to foreshortening friendships in order to please mates who never wanted to have friends around. If the effort is too great it may be that our focus has become more narrow, our world smaller; this may be our way of adapting to a lessened ability to deal with the stresses of life. Then only our children are safe. Only a few old friends are safe—even though we may quarrel with them or resent them fiercely because they remind us of our own limitations.

And yet, and yet: even older people who say they have no need for friends or whose actions make it seem as if they are wholly reclusive do, in their own way, reach out to others—sometimes in the most striking and eloquent ways. I recall a man in work clothes I met in that singles compound near Disneyland. While he was in his early sixties and not retired yet, he provides a vivid illustration of what I mean: surrounded by young singles as he was, he told me he knew no one there personally, simply worked and came home to his room and stayed there. Then why did he choose to live in that particular place? "Because it's convenient," he said in his taciturn way. Yet his decision to live in a lively singles apartment building was based on more than "convenience," since he could have very conveniently and for less money found a more conventional apartment. Here, however, he could live his loner's life while being surrounded by people, fulfilling his need for them in the only way in which he was capable.

And then there are some of the lonely, withdrawn people who gravitate to senior citizen centers in our major cities. At the Model Cities Senior Center in Washington, D.C., and at the Freda Mohr Center in Los Angeles, for instance—the first populated by low-income blacks, the second by lower-middle-class Jews—the identical phenomenon occurs: some talk to no one, participate in no songfests, no card games, no activities with others. Yet day after day they show up and sit, like that loner, surrounded by people. They are like young children who have not yet learned how to relate to other children; they do things by themselves, crocheting, perhaps, or playing solitaire—they are engaged in parallel play. At the Model Cities center a lady of about seventy-five comes in and follows the same routine every day: she arrives sometime in midmorning, smiles at everyone, then sits by herself and refuses to say anything to anyone for the rest of the day. About the same time each day, an elderly gentleman shows up, sits down next to her, and talks to her by the hour. She seems not to hear; he seems not to realize that she does not hear. Something, something is going on between them.

At Boston State Hospital, Dr. Ching-piao Chen has sensitively shaped a treatment modality called "social therapy"—the use of interpersonal relations—to reach geriatric and schizophrenic patients. What he did, simply, was to establish a "pub" in the hospital—a place where these withdrawn, traumatized patients could mingle with each other, drink beer, wine, or soft drinks, and maybe learn to care about themselves and others again. Eventually, they did begin to care, dressed more neatly, talked more, went to bed later, formed friendships, talked to each other about their pasts, about themselves and their feelings. Lifeless in what had been a lifeless institution, they produced a miracle: they made contact, touched each other, and in time many became well enough to be discharged into regular community nursing homes.

Some of us in our seventies and eighties delight in having younger friends as well as those in our own age group; most of us, in these later years, feel most comfortable with people more or less approximating our own ages. This has not so much to do with a narrowing of focus as it does with the realization that what we are experiencing—those physical, mental, and emotional changes that constitute the aging process—is as unique to us as the experience of childhood is to children, and of adolescence to adolescents. An eighty-year-old and a twenty-year-old can be friends, of course, but there are also psychic limits to that friendship if we view it as a friendship of equals. Beyond a certain point, they are no longer equals; if the relationship continues to deepen emotionally it takes on much more of the characteristics of a child-parent or child-grandparent relationship. How can the twenty-year-old, no matter how understanding, truly know what it means to have to grope for names, struggle with stiffening joints, feel sensual needs that seem mocked by our old persons' bodies? The twenty-year-old can empathize but, not having been there yet, cannot truly *know*. It is a comfort, sometimes, to be with a friend who does know. We don't need so many words: we recognize each other's fears and wants and other feelings because they are our own.

As Zena S. Blau stresses in her paper, our friendships have to be fairly consonant with our situations—we have to share central experiences in common with our friends—or the friendships are likely to be in trouble. This is true of the man who retires while all his cronies are still working, and of the man who continues working while his cronies are enjoying the leisurely life; of the widow or widower in a circle of married friends; of the married oldster in a circle of widows and widowers.

"The effect that changes in major status have on the friendships of older people depends on the *prevalence* of these changes in the social structure," Mrs. Blau concludes. "A change in status which places the individual in a deviant position in his age or sex group interfers with his opportunities to maintain old friendships."

In our neighborhoods, too, our friendships often suffer if we are deviants in relation to our neighbors. When sociologist Herbert J. Gans investigated the social life of Levittowners—residents of a new tract development in New Jersey—he found that some elderly people in the area could take on "quasi-grandparental roles toward the kids on the block, but others were lonely and uncomfortable among the young families," and the gardeners among them were upset by the children romping over their flowerbeds. Older persons living in city neighborhoods where there are few other people their age around are often lonely and neglected, especially as they get on in years and find it difficult because of finances or health to visit friends living in other sections of town. Most isolated of all are the aged living in high-crime areas; afraid to venture out after dark, possibly in ill health, they sit in numbing loneliness remembering better days.

Some gerontologists, city planners, and social critics have a "perfect world" vision: restructure our communities so that old and young, married and unmarried, can all live together in harmonious and enriching circumstances—the young helping the old keep youthful, the old preparing the young for what lies ahead. The main reasons the old segregate themselves now, the visionaries say, is because society devalues old age and trains the old not to depend on the young. Retirement communities, "lifetime care" centers, and other age-segregated facilities are anathema to them, and the more radical of the group would do away with such facilities altogether.

But visionaries sometimes lose sight of individual needs that do not conform to their vision, and in this case they forget that while some of us would not step within ten feet of a retirement community, others of us feel more comfortable in a setting in which we are surrounded by our age mates. Responsibilities individually assumed are one thing; responsibilities thrust upon us simply because we are older are as much of a way of stereotyping us as it would be to shove us all into rocking chairs.

Older men and women who choose to live in retirement communities or the like are not forced to move there; often, in fact, such communities entail quite a lot of expense. When I questioned a group of residents at Rossmoor Maryland, a community for middle-class adults situated in Silver Springs, Maryland, about half said that being with people in similar circumstances was an important factor influencing their decision to move there; of the rest, most said it had been at least a point in favor of the move. Most had come from suburban areas. "I felt I would be more accepted here," said a widow in her sixties. A married woman of about the same age said, "We lived in a high-rise for ten months and didn't meet a soul. But here we're always active with people, at the pool, for bridge or dinner parties." A few muttered about the "aura of old age." As one widower put it, "A lot of the talk is, 'Mrs. Smith was taken to the hospital,'" but they also indicated that in an imperfect world there are no perfect choices and they had chosen the best of the options available to them.

The point is that the more options we have available to us, including the existence of a wide variety of age-segregated as well as mixed communities, the better able we are to lead lives most congenial to us.

Maybe an unconscious reason some people are drawn to retirement communities is the fact that there are always new friends to choose from when old friends pass away. This is not meant in a cold-blooded way: the death of friends does not eliminate the need for friends. Actually, the reality of death is never far from our minds as we age because death does shrink our circle of friends and serves as an ever-present reminder of our own mortality. Some people are obsessed by this: they told me that the obituary column is the first thing they turn to in their daily newspapers, to see if any friends or acquaintances are mentioned. "It's too bad, all my friends seem to be kicking off," said a retired service station operator in a Boston suburb; with a little laugh he added, "I dunno—my number must be up."

The realization can numb us; the more of our friends who die, the more protective we may become of ourselves and of our feelings, to the point of removing ourselves somewhat emotionally from those that remain. An elderly lady in Minneapolis said, "When they first started passing on I used to grieve so much. But now I go to the funerals and it's much harder to cry. Old people don't have many tears left." But the reminder of death can evoke a rush of feeling, too. In a Cleveland suburb a tough old man, a retired newspaperman in his seventies, told me of a memorable experience that had occurred to him a few months earlier: a childhood friend from the West Coast, in town on a rush business trip, had stopped by briefly to see him. It had been twenty years since they had last seen or talked to each other. The sudden phone call from his old friend announcing his visit had thrilled my interviewee, and then—"don't get me wrong, I'm not effeminate, but when he left I felt this thing, this would be the last time we'd see each other and at the door I hugged him and kissed him on the cheek. I told him, 'This is the way I feel about you, Ed,' and he said he understood. I'd never ever done a thing like that before." Over and over again we prove that, even at seventy, and even if it is not the usual way with us, there are vulnerable times when we cannot help ourselves from reaching out in friendship.

THE PROCESS

10

From Stranger to Friend

"ONE of the charms of friendship," commented a debonair New Yorker, an investment counselor who has a long-standing feud going with most of his relatives, "is that you can bloody well choose your friends, not have them rammed down your throat by an accident of birth or marriage." Freedom of choice often is one of the distinctions drawn between friendship and kinship, but it is overdrawn. We have our choice of friends, of course, but our options are not as free as we might like to think.

First and most obvious, we are limited in our choice of friends by the boundaries of the worlds we live in. After all, we can only be friends with people as we encounter them; it follows that the more curtailed our environments are, the smaller is our pool of potential friends. The elderly lady who never strays more than a couple of blocks from her house has only the people on those two blocks to choose from if she wishes to make friends. The teenage son of an Army captain can only make friends with other army children if his parents confine their associations to the post. The clinical psychologist who devotes himself to his work may do a lot of traveling, may attend seminars, conferences, and the like, but still he is apt to meet only people in his own area of professional concern or in allied fields. The friends of most professionals tend to be other professionals.

Logically, certainly, the greater a person's occupational commitment, the greater the likelihood that most of his friends will be colleagues. A study bearing this out was conducted on dentists, advertising men, and college professors. The professors, devoted to their careers (some working sixty to seventy hours a week) and living in a college town where they were isolated from the nonacademic community, scored the highest in terms of numbers of colleague-friends. The dentists were least committed to their work; moreover, working alone and with only moderate participation in professional associations, they had the least number of colleague-friends. The ad men were somewhere in between.

Social and occupational mobility also is a factor limiting or enlarging our potential pool of friends. If we are mobile we encounter a more diverse group of people. We might retain a few friends from our original social stratum, as well as cultivating others on the level at which we have arrived. Otherwise we do not much stray from our own social class.

In fact, both age and social class are important factors limiting our choice of friends. Virtually every study made of such matters affirms that we are most likely to be closer to people in our general age group and on our general social level.

Not that there is never any crossing over. A number of my respondents mentioned age as an aspect they do not have in common with close friends: several middle-aged men and women, for instance, have friends ten or twenty years older or younger than they. But whereas someone in his forties can easily be seen as being involved in a deepening friendship with people in their thirties or sixties, say, it becomes more difficult to take at face value the words of a grandmother who said she numbered some teenagers among her friends. Undoubtedly her relationship with them is very warm and friendly, but must also be strongly imbued with the grandparent-grandchild flavor; because they are not friendships between equals they cannot ripen the way a friendship between two people sharing somewhat similar experiences in life can.

Frequently, when two people of very dissimilar ages or social classes do become friends, their relationship is strongly focused on an activity they enjoy together. A middle-aged man I know is friends with a boy of twelve; both build miniature sailboats and sail them on a lake in the park; they have long and earnest discussions about their hobby. An investment counselor and a building superintendent I know are friends, in the sense that both belong to the same aquarium club, where they get together once a month to discuss the raising of guppies, the diet of mollies, and how best to eradicate ich. But they have not been to each other's houses and the only contact they have with each other outside of club meetings is an occasional phone call.

Social class keeps us apart for several reasons. If social class is a measure of a person's worth, as it must be in a class society, then it follows that the higher the class the more the members of that class are going to formulate conventions to exclude members of lower classes. Most people would rather not talk about their investment in snobbism; they zero in on life-styles. And it is true that styles of life—interests, values, attitudes, what one enjoys doing—often vary quite a bit between differing classes. This need not only revolve around money and what it is one can afford to do. Lower-class and middle-class mothers involved in school activities are sometimes at odds, sometimes find themselves speaking quite different languages, because their attitudes toward discipline in particular and child rearing in general are divergent. A busy construction man and a social-work-agency head may live on the same block but, in terms of life-styles, be in different worlds.

Life-styles flow out of values and values suggest life-styles. "Friendship may be shortly defined, 'a perfect conformity of opinion upon all religious and civil subjects, united with the highest degree of mutual esteem and affection,' " Cicero said, and while most of us would probably agree that we do not need a "perfect conformity" in order to be able to trust and enjoy each other, some consonance of values and beliefs is very important. It eliminates an important source of friction. It affirms for us that what we think is good, is worthwhile, is significant. At various times children, Job Corpsmen, college students, schizophrenics, alcoholics, and surgical patients have been tested by social psychologists to find out just what kinds of strangers they were most attracted to. Across the board, children, Job Corpsmen, college students, schizophrenics, alcoholics, and surgical patients all came out of the tests showing that they were attracted to strangers in proportion to the values they share in common with those strangers. In sum, we are most drawn to people who are like ourselves in certain fundamental ways.

Of course, we hardly present an attitude scale to each person we meet—to each stranger who has the potential of becoming an acquaintance who has the potential of becoming a friend. But we are constantly involved in a kind of weeding-out process merely by virtue of the milieus in which we find ourselves. The factory worker is not apt to socialize in the executive halls. An arch conservative is not likely to join a political club oriented to liberal or radical politics. People without children in the schools do not join the PTA. Bigots do not make friends with the kinds of persons they are bigoted against. Moreover, the moment a conversation begins all kinds of signals and cues, verbal and nonverbal, are at once exchanged that let each of the two parties know something about the other, something of the hidden as well as of the overt person; thus we pick up nuances, we begin to sense whether this is "our kind" of person or not.

As an intriguing paper on friendship as a social process elaborates, most of the time when some discordance is felt, when we sense that someone is not "our kind," then "the possible beginnings of friendship are nipped in the bud." A gross and aboveboard instance is the case of the vociferously pro-black white woman who antagonizes all the anti-black white women in her apartment building; she is automatically excluded, and excludes herself, from the possibility of friendship with them.

So our prejudices and biases further reduce our pool of potential friends (except in those instances where our biases are weaker than our interest in a particular person). And biases are at work long before anybody says a word about his viewpoints—or about anything else, for that matter. Negative first impressions formed merely by looking at a person eliminate at least some people from our pool of potential friends; we simply don't cross the room—at a party, say—to talk with them. One of my interviewees vowed that he never makes friends with people who have dirty fingernails "because those nails tell me all about them that I care to know." For some visually oriented men and women the clothes a person wears immediately make an impact, favorable or unfavorable: "It is," a magazine art director commented, "the most immediate environment around a person." Many of my respondents, but more women than men, referred to eyes and mouths as features they notice first on people and are influenced by. Of course, negative first impressions can turn positive if we see a person frequently enough to discover likable traits, but often we do not get that far.

But we are not so simple in our functioning as to be favorably disposed only to people who by their looks, attitudes, or actions remind us favorably of ourselves. For one thing, an irrational element not infrequently is at work in our reactions to people. Somebody's background and attitudes may coincide remarkably with mine, and I may still say to myself, "I don't like him," or, "I don't trust him," or, "That's nobody I'd care to know." There may be an obvious reason insofar as I'm concerned—this person looks cruel, or maybe he comes across as pretty boring—but then again it may be just a visceral reaction with nothing concrete to peg it on. But then why do I feel that way? Maybe he reminds me of someone long forgotten with whom I went through some unpleasantness; who knows? Such feelings are hard to pin down even with careful thought. The man I instantly don't like may simply have the shape of face of someone who gave me a hard time in the dim past, something as vague as that. Then again, he may even remind me of myself without my realizing it—that is, remind me of those aspects of myself I don't care for and would rather not be faced with. Most difficult for all of us to cope with in our relationships with others is their negative aspects that mirror negatives in our own personalities.

Often we are favorably disposed to friends of friends—or think we are—but find the spark of attraction to be conspicuously absent even at first meeting. If we feel close to certain people, why wouldn't we feel close to those people's other friends? Maybe unconscious jealousy plays a role: a person's attention and affection are scarce goods, and if two people want it from a third, they may feel competitive toward each other. But surely the fact that we're many-sided in our personalities is a crucial reason: Joe has something to offer my friend Ted; I have something different to offer my friend Ted; Ted is obviously nourished by his association with us both, but Joe may not be drawn to my sensitivities nor I to his. So we leave each other somewhat cold, or neutral at best—and each of us, forgetting for a moment that Ted is not our mirror image, may even wonder what he sees in the other.

First impressions comprise the initial phase of the friendship process. If they are favorable, what happens next? That depends on the social structure in which the relationship began. If the initial encounter is a professional one, say, and then it happens that we keep on running into each other or work on a project together, we build up a history of interaction that eventually reaches the point of friendship (maybe). In any event, the repeated contacts we have with each other as a result of a shared project or activity are natural and—in that sense—effortless.

Alternatively, we meet somebody in a social situation of some kind—a party, say—and there is generalized liking of each person for the other. It would be nice, we think, to see those persons again. We may even exchange phone numbers and promise to be in touch. But while many friendships are made in just this way, it is a mode strewn with pitfalls. Somebody has to make the effort. Who is going to make it first? It may be that neither person really is an initiator, that the initial contact hasn't provided enough of a motivation to overcome diffidence, and that each leaves it to the other to make the call.

To make that call, to arrange something, takes effort. Effort means energy, means time. When it comes to energy, many of us take the path of least resistance. Many of us are busy and active; our lives are crowded with people as it is. Work, family life, existing friends, leisure-time activities occupy us. And while those people we meant to have over really were very nice, days slip by, weeks pass; the longer we refrain from making another contact, the slimmer the chance that we will ever get together again, except perhaps coincidentally. The longer the time that goes by, the less important another meeting seems. Occasionally, for whatever reason, the image of a person or a couple I'd met some time before and had wanted to see again but never got around to pops into my head. Then, for just a few minutes, I feel a twinge of something akin to sadness: "What have I missed?"—followed by blunt realism: "If I'd *really* wanted to, wouldn't I have made the time?" Time, time, always time. So often we use the excuse of time to cover feelings of apathy or diffidence. Anyway, the graveyard of social relationships is littered with the bones of friendships that might have been.

When we do make the effort to see each other again, an invitation usually revolves around an activity that will allow us to get to know each other better: drinks, maybe, or lunch, or a dinner party. If we don't want to be isolated with these new people the first or second time around, if we consider it too much of a risk, we include old friends—or invite the new acquaintances to a party at which there are a lot of other people. Whatever the form, though, we are now engaged in the initial phases of a testing and exploring process. We don't quite put it that way; we do not say, "Hey, the Joneses seem like a nice couple, let's have them over, feel them out, test them, see if we get along—if they measure up to our standards and fill our needs." Nevertheless, something of the sort goes on as we move from being strangers to being friends. It occurs too when we are thrown together more naturally, as in colleague relationships or perhaps in neighborhood situations—but in a less studied fashion, less self-consciously.

Like the courting stage of a new romance—which in some ways it resembles—this is a special time, a specially exciting time. Slowly, or not so slowly, things emerge: likes and dislikes. Favorite foods. The kinds of movies and music we enjoy—or do not enjoy. Hobbies. Sports. Something about our respective styles and sensitivities and intelligence. Value-related facets of our personalities emerge. All the little brushstrokes that, put together, add up to portraits of ourselves, more clearly visible each time we see each other.

There is more self-revelation, consciously and unconsciously. Suddenly, maybe, we begin talking about topics of deeper significance to us—childhood memories, for instance. As this mutual exploration continues we gain a warm and growing awareness that what we are saying is understood—yes, *understood*—by the other. This is how trust and intimacy develop. It has been suggested that people are actually involved in more intimate or personal conversations when first getting to know each other than later on. More likely, the intimate exchanges are more concentrated at first, when we are especially intent on perceiving each other's humanity.

We are not only discovering similarities—that being the more overt part of the process—we are also finding out whether we complement each other, whether the total "fit" between us is good. Though social psychologists hold differing theories of attraction— some say we are drawn to people like us, others say opposites attract—it is more probable that both dimensions operate concurrently as we are drawn to certain persons and not to others. Similarities probably create an instant aura of sympathy between ourselves and our potential friends: by our recognizing ourselves in them they become less strange (less fearsome?); the climate of goodwill thus generated enables us to explore each other on more complicated and subtle levels.

Complementariness is among those levels. It explains how the shy, sensitive person and the more outgoing, thicker-skinned person find each other, for instance—each draws on the other's strengths. We "take" from others what we individually lack. Sometimes, as in the case of the shier and the more outgoing person, or the more assertive and the more submissive, complementariness is glaringly obvious. But it does not have to be. Sometimes traits or needs are held in common by the two friends, but are far more pronounced or stronger in the one person than in the other. Two people who are aggressive talkers have a lot in common, but are hardly apt to be drawn to each other in friendship —they would always be competing with each other for the right to talk. One who is better at talking and another who talks well but is better at listening are much more apt to be compatible. Both similarities and opposites can attract—or, depending on what they are, repel.

Testing and exploring is an inevitable process in any new relationship, but the process varies with the individuals concerned, in terms of both time and intensity. It can be quick, over with in a matter of weeks or even days (when everything is artificially speeded up, as when two vacationers meet). With people who move slowly and cautiously in relation to other people, it can last a year or longer. Most of the people who talked to me about their friendships said that generally it takes them "a few months" to form a friendship. More men than women said they made friends very quickly (maybe because male-male friendships are apt to be more activity-oriented); more women than men said it takes them a long time (maybe because women disclose more of themselves in their friendships).

Many would-be friendships end almost before they have begun. It takes us little time to realize the fit is wrong; we do not pursue relationships with people with whom we basically feel incompatible. Often we are not motivated to pursue friendships with people who leave us feeling neutral about them, but sometimes people do pursue them, when there is no one around whom they would more clearly prefer. They figure that it is better to share things or do things with someone they feel tepid about than with no one at all. Such friendships usually only last until someone better does come along.

As for instant friendships, unless they are strongly activity-oriented they have much less of a chance to endure than those formed over time. We do need the time to learn each other's styles and quirks—otherwise, in our initial rush of enthusiasm, we tend to idealize the friend and idealization invariably invites a painful letdown. Impulsivity is not the handmaiden of constancy.

So we go about the process of sorting out the relationship, settling into the patterns that are appropriate to it. Signs tell us that we have moved from the stage of being simple acquaintances. We want to be together more. We intrude into each other's thoughts more. There is growing warmth between us. We find it less imperative to cover up our thoughts and feelings; we can relax more, feel more spontaneous, in each other's presence. We can afford silences when we are together; it is not necessary to be "on" all the time. We feel freer to ask favors of each other; to do favors for each other; increasingly, we feel that dimension of trust that means we can "count on" each other. We find that, as we get to know each other better, words become less important—we know enough about each other to take shortcuts; we can "read" each other, sense each other's thoughts or moods more. We have incorporated ourselves, my friend and I, each into the other's psyche.

These are elements present in all our friendships to some degree; it is precisely the degree to which they are present that gives the friendship its flavor and defines it. There are friends who remain at a level that is little more than "friendly acquaintanceship." We enjoy chatting when we run into each other on the street, say, and maybe get together once or twice or three times a year. But the investment we have in each other is relatively minimal; we have little "right" to take each other's time or ask each other for help; we are more formal in each other's presence; we trust each other more than if we were strangers or fresh acquaintances, but not much more. "Casual friends" would define people we see more often and relate to more warmly, or people we see as seldom as we do "friendly acquaintances" but are more emotionally involved with. "Good friends" and "close friends" denote progressively warmer and more involved relationships, while "intimates" are the ones with whom we have the deepest relationships: the barriers between us are at the lowest level we are capable of managing; these are our best friends, like family, or like family we wish we'd had.

Of course, few of us may use such terms or their equivalent to describe our friends—but the feelings behind the terms is what counts, and those feelings do cause us to differentiate at least between close friends and the ones who are not so close, guiding our behavior.

Something every friendship also has to some degree is ritual. Seemingly, we have always needed ritual to stabilize us (reassure us?) in our affairs; modern times are no different, the friendship tie is no different. So we tend to regularize our relationships in certain ways. We meet for lunch on Tuesdays or play bridge on Friday nights or have two-family outings once a month. Or, even if we don't meet on a regular schedule, we do the same enjoyable things each time we do get together. Or our talk falls into a familiar pattern: shop talk, catching up on things, gossip, whatever. The telephone is not only a great instrument for keeping in touch, it is a great instrument for keeping ritually in touch. How we relate to each other—the style between us—can easily have ritualistic overtones: for instance, two guys, the best of friends, always kidding each other. Secret signs, codes, and signals are obviously ritualistic; the secrets that two friends share can have a ritualistic aspect to them. The exchange of Christmas cards between two friends who have not seen each other for a long time—which is sometimes criticized as being a meaningless exercise—can, depending on the feelings that go into the exchange, be a ritual way each friend has of saying, "Let's not cut the tie between us." There is nothing meaningless about that.

11

Constancy and Change

IN a world of ever-present change we want some constancy. From friendship we want—we expect—a significant measure of both constancy and consistency. It is, in fact, one of the rewards we derive from the relationship: this is my friend, this is someone I can count on, to show up on the handball court every Thursday evening as we've arranged, or to enjoy baked Alaska with because he is a lover of good food, or to be receptive to an account of my problems because we have become each other's confidants, or to hang on the phone for hours with me chatting away about things that stimulate us, or otherwise to present himself to me in the accustomed way. We make leeway for off days, bad moods, and depressions, of course. But most of us would find it too disconcerting to carry on for very long relationships with friends who were different people each time we met them; we would come to doubt our own reality in the end.

A measure of our need for constancy and consistency is the very fact that we categorize our friendships, even if we do so only in the grossest of terms like "casual" and "close." To categorize a relationship is to define it, so we know where we stand, so we know how to behave in ways appropriate to it, so we know what to expect. The extent to which we set up these ground rules has to do with a facet of our personalities—with the extent to which we are or are not rigid. But even very flexible people differentiate—even they come to expect different things from the relationships with casual and close friends. Otherwise "casual" and "close" would have no meaning and we would end up being very confused.

Fundamental to any other expectations we may have is the expectation that in any given friendship our own view of the relationship and our friend's view are reasonably consonant. If we and our friends assess things very differently our expectations will of course be divergent. Since expectations are grounded in needs, our needs therefore are not likely to be mutually met, a perfect situation for conflict. A utility executive who prefers distance in his relationships told me how upset he was when his golfing partner, with whom he had never discussed anything more intimate than sports, suddenly "blurted out a lot of very personal stuff about his marriage and his sex life." Paradoxically, self-revelation is one of the most powerful forces for the deepening of a relationship, but only when the atmosphere is congenial to one's opening up. In this case it was inappropriate both to the occasion and to the relationship, and my respondent was unable to handle it. Conversely, a magazine editor told me how upset he was when his closest friend, a man he had gone to high school with, withheld from him the fact that he had cancer "until he was practically on his deathbed. I tried to respect that; I know he was suffering and had his own reasons for not telling me, but—it sounds terrible, I know, but I was hurt . . . like he'd let me down."

We expect some consistency in terms of liking, too. Friends do not have to like each other equally well for their relationship to be satisfactory to both, as long as both recognize and accept the situation. If, however, the friend who likes more goes on and on about what a wonderful friendship he has with the friend who likes less, the latter is apt to feel very uncomfortable (guilty?) and remove himself further. Several of my respondents mentioned that people they hardly knew referred to them as good friends, even dear friends. They found it odd; while some were sensitive to the tremendous need for contact that must have prompted those acquaintances to mislabel the relationship, none liked it.

Another way we show the extent to which we depend on this assurance of constancy and consistency in our friendship is the fact that we type our friends. Visionaries have always held that the only type of friendship worth pursuing is the all-encompassing one. Visionaries have always been generalists in the art of friendship; as Aristotle said, "There meet in it all the qualities that friends should have." But very early in life we learn that in the real world no single friend can be everything to us, can share all our interests, fancies, and moods. Some of the most intense adolescent best-friendships may be an exception, but those relationships are generally short-lived and punctuated by heartbreak: "You aren't living up to my expectations." No, we are not generalists, we are specialists; we take stock of our friends, as it were, matching parts of them with parts of us. "Different friends for different wants," as one of my respondents charmingly put it.

The more varied our interests, obviously, the wider our circle of friends. One couple I interviewed belongs to a bullfight club and has aficionado friends they do not see outside the club; they have other friends they travel with; friends they share their respective hobbies with; a couple of neighbor friends and friends from the husband's work place; and two or three sets of friends who fit no special classification except the ones of being fun to be and talk with. When they throw parties they hardly ever mix their friends. Maybe this couple is at an extreme but even when our friendships are not so sharply focused on interests and activities, when we simply have a bunch of good friends we enjoy being with and relaxing with, we still tend to specialize somewhat. This one has a sharp sense of humor, that one can talk sports best, the third is most open and perceptive, and then there are the family friends we click best with as families.

"This one makes me feel good one way and that one makes me feel good another way," said a lady in Baltimore. Certainly, many people have individual friends who are multifaceted friends, who play many roles in their lives and with whom they share many facets of their respective selves—closest friends they enjoy being with the most. But unless we are what Dr. Stanton Peele of

Harvard University felicitously calls "people-addicted"—unless we cling to one special person to the exclusion of the rest of the world—we are still going to seek out other people at times. We may not know exactly why we have the impulse to see a certain friend at a certain time. We may simply be "in the mood" to do so. That mood, even if we cannot describe it clearly, is our typing-and-selection process at work. As that Baltimore lady said, "Different friends for different wants."

One remarkable way in which we type our friends is in the case of summer friendships. I encountered quite a few people who rent or own summer houses and who have marvelously enjoyable friendships with other regular vacationers in the same area—but who rarely see their summer friends except in summer, even if the year round they live no farther than across town from each other. Why? Well, the most usual answer I got was, "We're so busy with our other friends, we don't have time." It seemed like an insufficient answer, and while no one specifically articulated it, as I pursued the subject a more basic reason emerged. It looks as though we have a need to make the summer experience something special, to have the feeling that it provides a different texture to our lives than does the day-to-day routine. If summer friends—those friends we associate with a unique, relaxing, carefree time—become year-round friends, the summer experience would lose some of its specialness. Too, there may be specific things we enjoy doing with our summer friends that cannot carry over into winter, but I think we deliberately limit the range of interaction we have with them.

When our work and the rest of our lives are somewhat of a piece, we make few distinctions between "work friends" and "regular friends." Professionals often have easy social relationships with some of their colleagues at work. But if we make a sharp distinction between work and the other aspects of our lives, then work friends—much as they brighten our lives at work—remain just work friends; we rarely if ever see them casually outside the work place (except maybe for a regular organized activity like a bowling league). It was a distinct minority of blue-collar workers, for instance, who said they saw their work friends even occasionally on weekends. They talked of spending time with family and a few close "outside friends"—intimating that there was not room in their lives for socializing with the friends they saw at work. Again, there seems to be more to it than that: work friends satisfy certain needs distinctly related to the work place; work may be our least satisfying experience, in which case we want to put everything connected with it behind us at quitting time. Then again, we may feel that we don't want our work friends to get to know our families too well, and vice versa—because when we have been exploited most of our lives a basic precept we learn to live by in all situations is, "What others don't know won't hurt me."

The process of typing friends holds true even for the friends who act as our confidants. "Confidants" are generally thought of as people who listen to all our troubles. Sometimes they are. But among those of my interviewees who said they could unburden themselves to their friends were many who did not mean one friend, one confidant. They didn't automatically assume that just because a friend was close and trusted they could talk about anything with that person. They recognized that friends are first of all people, and people differ in their experiences, sensibilities, and prejudices, and that as a result they are more or less receptive to certain life problems and situations. My respondents went to those friends they felt would be most receptive and sensitive with regard to the issue at hand. Other friends were not necessarily excluded, but not relied upon for in-depth counsel.

We assume that our friends will be consistent in terms of the attributes that drew us to them in the first place. We do not expect the kind and gentle friend to become cruel, the generous friend to turn greedy, the articulate friend to become dull, the playful friend to become morose, the honest friend to turn untrustworthy. We accept the fact that people have lapses in which they are "not themselves," but if the change becomes a way of life and they are "themselves" in a new fashion we become very distressed. In part we are distressed by what we see as the deterioration of a friend, in part because we have suffered a psychological loss.

When friends change in ways that matter greatly to us—and it would matter, of course, if the change revolved around characteristics that attracted us in the first place—then we really suffer the possibility of incurring a multiplicity of losses. There were strengths we had in common, which meant that we saw our strengths reflected by the other, confirmed by the other; now that confirmation may be gone. Perhaps there were ways we complemented each other; now that symmetry is awry. We shared values; in the sharing we were both reinforced in our beliefs; now we may have lost that reinforcement. In fact, sometimes a friend changes in certain ways that can leave us feeling a little vulnerable, as though this is something happening too close to home. "I tried to talk her out of it but she wouldn't listen," said a teenager in Brooklyn about her erstwhile best friend, who was sleeping around with a lot of boys. "Finally I figured if I kept hanging around her people would say the same things about me that they said about her." A factory foreman in Minneapolis told of what happened when his best friend became an alcoholic: "I talked and talked, but couldn't get through to him. He became—well, a common drunk is the name for it, and that did it as far as our friendship was concerned."

Friendships require mutual respect, friendships require mutual acceptance. Those two facets go hand in hand. As we become friends we become cognizant not only of each other's strong points, the points we admire and respect, but of each other's warts and blemishes as well. The longer we get to know each other the more exposed we become—as much by what is not said as by what is, as much by nonverbal cues and nuances as by straightforward statements and actions. Nobody is perfect; we accept each other's faults. There is a great deal of security in knowing that. Almost all of the people I interviewed were emphatic about preferring to have their good friends know their faults as well as their virtues; as a theatrical designer a bit theatrically explained, "I feel best protected when I'm totally exposed." While none of us ever is "totally exposed," the principle holds. But there is the point: we accept faults in our friends—but the faults we accept most readily are those we have come to know. If a friend suddenly changes the ground rules on us, as it were, acquiring or allowing to emerge blemishes we had no idea were there, it can produce a lot of conflict and bring an end to the relationship as it did in the case of the newly promiscuous girl and the alcoholic man.

In sum, we only accept each other up to a point. It is never "My friend right or wrong." It is always "My friend despite the fact that he's wrong—unless I find his 'wrong' personally unbearable."

"A man's relationship to his friends is a sphere where important aspects of his personality are revealed," wrote Ernest Jones, Freud's biographer. He should have added, "A woman's, too." The kinds of friends we choose as well as the kinds of friends we eventually leave mirror what we are, what we have been, and perhaps what we would like to be. Extremes in friendship are always revealing, always a sign of past sorrow and present anxiety. Take some of the men and women brought up by emotionally cold, withdrawn parents: they keep friends at a safe distance always—or always cling to friends with heartbreaking desperation. Take some of the men and women whose home life was such that they never got over their infant fear of strangers: grown-up, they need to be as alike as Siamese twins with their friends in thought, action, and even appearance. Take some of the men and women who were psychically undernurtured or never nurtured as children: never having been given to, they refuse to give, to do favors, when they are involved in adult relationships; or, feeling worthless, they can only extend favors but never accept them; or, in trying to make up for what had been, they seek endless favors from friends—as proof of affection.

We are not so very different in the way we behave with family and with friends. The warmhearted, generous husband is almost surely also the warmhearted, generous friend. The patient, understanding father is generally patient and understanding with his friends. Conversely, the man who bosses his wife or mistress around is also domineering with his friends, though in such situations the dynamics involved are sometimes more complex. The man who has a wife to boss around may not need to boss his friends (though he is not apt to latch on to friends as aggressive as he); if he loses his wife, however, and has no one else to dominate, his friends will feel the full brunt of his vigor. At times it is only through the reaction of his friends that a person is able to see what he is doing to his family. At the Family Service Association of Nassau County, New York, Associate Director Robert Sunley told me of a case like that: the client was a very exploitative man, always taking advantage of people, family included. Though his marriage was suffering he projected so many of his own neurotic reactions onto his wife that he was totally unable to see his own part in the drama. But then his friends, also subject to his exploitative urges, began to move away from him. Because they were not as closely involved with him as his family was, he was able to be more objective in their case, seeing through their withdrawal what he was doing to others of importance in his life.

It is not true, as is sometimes thought, that people who are isolated from kin make a lot of friends to compensate, and that people with loads of relatives have little interaction with friends. While this happens in individual cases the reverse seems to hold true in terms of broad societal patterns: people isolated from kin tend also to be isolated from friendship; the outgoing family person is also likely to be outgoing in terms of friends.

The way we conduct our friendships illuminates some of the more hidden aspects of our selves. Dependency—often a sensitive issue—is a case in point. "My friends are always so dependent on me. I know I'm strong, and usually I enjoy helping them—but sometimes it gets to be too much," a middle-aged woman in Minneapolis said and believed. She was speaking the truth, but it was only part of the truth: when the friends we choose all run to a kind we can feel superior to one way or another, we must unconsciously be inviting that kind—and, maybe slyly, maybe unwittingly, encouraging their dependency. *Their* dependency— but what about our own needs in that direction? Are we denying them? A man from Illinois, not yet thirty and not married, seemed very bent in that direction; he wrote, "While I have always wanted friends, I have not wanted to feel that I *need* them. Only those who are truly independent, I think, are worth having as friends. I find, to my disappointment, that I need friends—communication with them—when I have suffered any sort of emotional reverse or depression. I require them then not necessarily to discuss the problem, but merely to take my mind off the situation." Which is another way of saying, "I need you, but I don't want to need you, so I'll camouflage my need for you."

And four times, five times, perhaps a bit oftener, I heard men (it was always men) blurt out quite seriously, "Our best friends are our mothers." It does seem like another way of saying, "I want to be taken care of and have all my needs met without working to have it happen, the way they were met when I was a baby. My mother is the only person I can really trust." Paradoxically, if these men had been able to trust their mothers way back then, they would have an easier time trusting other people now.

We want constancy in our friendships but, paradoxically, aren't always ready to be constant. That is, our need to be with friends can wax and wane somewhat, and not only because we may be at different stages of our life cycles. Creative people, for example, sometimes need periods of solitude when in the throes of creative endeavors; their energies then in the main go into, and their psychic nourishment principally comes from, the work in progress. When we are going through an especially intense period of internal change and growth we often become less sociable, turn inward the better to get in touch with our feelings. When we emerge from this period of introspection it is to embrace the warmth of friends again, perhaps more intensely for a time, testing ourselves anew, and testing our "new" selves in their presence.

I know that when something wonderful has happened to me and my body tingles with the delight of it I want to call all my friends and tell them—share my happiness with them; I need them much more then. I know that when I am moody or depressed I tend to withdraw, to nurse my wounds alone, as it were, before reaching out for help—maybe also feeling, during the gloomiest periods, that I'm not a worthy recipient of the solace of friends. Judging from the responses of a number of my interviewees, I am hardly alone in this reaction to distress. They, too, talked about withdrawing at such times. We expect our friends to respect and understand this necessity of ours to be alone—and perhaps to intrude appropriately when we have been alone too long. It is all a matter of timing; this is where the sensitivity of friends, each in relation to the other, comes into play. Sometimes it doesn't work well, of course: a lady from a smallish town in Missouri wrote a little bitterly about a tragedy in her life "when I found well-meaning friends an annoyance. They kept trying to get me to talk about it and I really didn't want to talk about it."

Yet a number of other people told me of reaching out much more needfully to friends in the face of tragedy, something especially true of young people in reaction to the death of a parent. But not only young people: the moment his wife died after a lingering illness, a middle-aged man I know reacted, in the first heartbreaking moments, by calling all of his friends, right down the list, to announce the news. He was not being macabre; he needed to know, just then, that at least some of his world, the world of caring friends, was still intact.

We assume (or take for granted) that the kinds of relationship patterns we build up with friends, mutually gratifying as they are when we settle into them, will always stay that way. Of course, it is not something we should take for granted; that people grow away from each other is probably the top reason why friendships end. The more flexibility there is to the relationship the less risk there is of that happening, however, because then it becomes easier for us to accept divergencies—there is so much more going for us. The more narrowly focused and rigidly defined our relationship is, the more vulnerable change makes it.

Take Sarah and Jill, two unhappy divorcees: lonely misery drew them together. They clung to each other for support. Sufficiently healed after a time, Jill reached for the outside world again, encouraging Sarah to do the same. But Sarah could not, would not; instead she panicked, became very possessive with Jill, and the relationship ended.

Take Bill and Len: Bill was the leader, Len the follower in a relationship that worked well until Len went into therapy and emerged stronger, more individualistic, not so ready to follow any more. But Bill had not changed; he still needed to feel in charge and could not adapt to the new Len. "You're different," he said bitterly, not appreciatively, and turned away. He could no longer dominate, no longer feel superior to his friend.

As we talked, or as they filled out their friendship question-naire, some respondents who had never really thought about it very much began to realize that they were, or had been, caught up in rigid friendship patterns. It can be a thought-provoking discovery. "I am perhaps too eager to put myself out for a friend," wrote a male physician from a small northeastern state. "Maybe I am only comfortable if they are in my debt. I find it very difficult to ask a favor of a friend." A married illustrator, a woman in her twenties also from the Northeast, wrote, "There was a time when I wanted very much to please people, and I had a great need to feel I had friends and was appreciated. This wasn't very satisfactory since I wasn't really pleasing myself. So then there was a time when I concentrated on getting to know people very different from myself, but during this period other aspects of my life became unsteady. In reaching out toward friends then I found that I was essentially on the wrong track, whereupon everything turned upside down and the world seemed very dark indeed. But somehow or other I survived and discovered when I had reestablished my sense of perspective that I really did have a few very fine friends, and that we had been drawn toward one another simply by being ourselves and not making a great effort."

We want constancy and consistency, but we are always in the midst of change—dramatic change as in the case of that young woman or slow, imperceptible alterations of character. This suggests the existence of a kind of tension between the wish for constancy and the reality of change. And that in turn means we are always feeling each other out a bit, usually beneath the threshold of awareness, in a continuation of the testing-exploring process that is such a powerful element in the earliest stages of a friendship: where am I as a person just now and where are you? What impact have the other events in our lives made on us and how do they affect our relationship? Will we understand each other the way we used to? At this point what can we expect from and reveal to and give each other? I don't mean to suggest that we are in a constant state of uncertainty with our friends or they with us—merely that this continual redefining of the relationship is one of the many levels—a "hidden dynamic"—of it.

There is another kind of testing that friends sometimes engage in, but more overtly. Taking their cue from Ecclesiasticus—"If thou wouldst get a friend, try him before thou takest him, and do not credit him easily"—they say, "You don't really know somebody's a friend till you put him to the test." Matter-of-factly this is certainly so: we don't really know what anybody is going to do in any particular situation until the situation arises. But it may also be a way of saying, "I want to take all the risk out of my relationships." Which is impossible: even persons who "prove" themselves in one situation may not—or may not be able to—in another. Genuine commitment rests on faith, not proof.

If we do not help when a friend needs help it may be selfishness on our part, it may be thoughtlessness, it may be that we are not really as committed to the relationship as we (and the friend) had thought. But even the best of friends cannot always help each other, and when they cannot it may be difficult for all concerned. "This friend needed money at the same time I was not in a position to give any; this created strain and the friendship eventually faded," a retired public official reported; and a young man, referring to a close friend who still is close, said, "He was feeling low and needed a big boost, but I was going through a hard time too just then, and couldn't do anything for him. Well, we fought about it and didn't see each other for a time, but then we had a good talk and that cleared the air." Friends "should" help friends —but "should" is such a locked-in word, removed from real-life feelings and events. A few of my respondents referred to friendships they had to pull out of to save themselves: they had helped and helped misfortune-prone friends and found they had no role left to play in life save that of ministering angel. "It became too draining," said a nurse in upstate New York, and a Los Angeles doctor proudly announced that it had taken him a long time to learn, but that he was finally able to say no as well as yes.

We don't really know what we will do in any given circumstance until it is upon us; neither do we know what the friendship, in its entirety, will bring. Friendship is a voyage of discovery, as is life itself; there is no way of knowing, at the outset, how it will go and where it will take us. We cannot predict ahead of time what joys, what pleasures or disappointments, we shall encounter. In defining friends as "casual" or "close" we are voicing expectations, but there are times when the unexpected—in the form of a gift of self—prompts a striking redefinition of the relationship. A man's son, involved in a car accident, was near death; one of the man's "close" friends, upon hearing the news, said, "Oh, I'm so sorry, now let me tell you what's happened to me . . ."—while a "casual" friend, unbidden, came over several times being wonderfully supportive. Yes, the "close" friend is a friend no more; the "casual" friend has become close. A woman threw a cocktail party for a person she described as a "moderately good friend" shortly before the friend's wedding; during the party, suddenly, the friend's fiancé died on the spot of a heart attack, and now—"We stayed together the whole night, I held her—we're like sisters now."

Terrible circumstances can put us into loving contact—and wonderful happenings can tear our friendships apart. A friend's success is, in fact, one of the most difficult situations that faces any friendship. This is especially true when the two friends have always identified closely with each other, for then a welter of conflicting emotions come into play: my friend publishes a song, wins the lottery, gets a fancy promotion, writes a runaway best seller, marries someone wonderful and rich . . . my friend has done it; I rejoice. I am like my friend, it could happen to me; I rejoice. But it didn't happen to me, only to my friend; I feel a loss of self-esteem. We were alike, neither better than the other, but now—for me, a loss of self-esteem. My friend has done it, will he reject me now? (And so it happens at times that the left-behind friend rejects the suddenly successful friend first.) On the successful friend's part, too, there are contradictory emotions . . . I'm truly sorry it didn't happen to him . . . but I'm glad it happened to me . . . but I want things to be the same between us . . . but is he looking at me enviously? . . . but I'll see him often, show him there is nothing different between us . . . but guess it's time to start thinking about moving into a bigger house. It all depends on which of the feelings predominate. Sometimes friendships survive intact; not infrequently they don't.

We cannot predict how the friendship will evolve, nor can we tell whether it will materially affect our lives. I am thinking of my friend Jack H.: he introduced me to a young woman who, it later turned out, would be my wife. How were Jack and I to know, when we first became friends, that he would be instrumental in my marrying? Jack introduced me to somebody, but it was a quirk of fate more than a turning point in my life resulting from the effects of the friendship itself. As for turning points, very few of my respondents could point to such dramatic changes occurring from the influence of the friendship itself. A psychologist referred to the crucial role a friend had played, when he was in his early thirties, in his decision to change professions. A young legal secretary spoke of a friend who first involved her in the women's movement, and which "changed my whole life." There were a couple of others.

Yet a number of people spoke about turning points resulting from friendships in another sense: no single striking event occurred, they said, but particular friendships had cumulative effects on their lives, profoundly affecting them. There was the graduate student, her background in a military family, who is now living happily in a communal situation as the result of a friend's influence. There was the young woman, now married, who talked about her friendship with a married couple at a time when she was single and cynical: "I learned from them that marriage can be realistic and extremely satisfying. . . . It was my first exposure to a marriage that differed from my parents' and had more influence on my decisions about marriage than I realized at the time." A man in his fifties, a deputy clerk, credited "much of what I think I have in the way of taste, responsibility to myself, and acceptance for the consequences of my behavior" to his association with a few good friends. And there was the legal secretary who recalled a lonely childhood as a sickly girl, having to relate mainly to adults and never really learning a casual give-and-take with peers: "I was pretty much of a loner in high school. When I got to college I had trouble relating to my peer group. My college roomie (from a big family) with real patience and skill 'socialized' me, so to speak, and probably was responsible for keeping me from going back to the 'protection' of home."

Friendships change, we change, the friendship changes us—but the change we least expect, at least until our older years, is death. The death of a very good friend is a shocker: we have laughed and fought with each other, we have gotten to understand each other and go along with each other's quirks, we have built up a *history* together, and now it is at an end. It is a shocker: in youth an event so bizarre as to be unreal; in middle age, accompanied by the realization, "Now it begins"; in old age grim news bringing the inevitable question, "Who's next?" We grieve for our friend, we confront the reality of our own mortality, we suffer the loss—well, the loss of self in the other. "I poured so much into that sonofabitch," mourned a young man, just out of high school, whose best friend had died in an accident the month before. "Now, why'd he have to go and die for?" We have other friends, good friends, close friends, but each friendship is a thing of its own; no two friends can take each other's places and no two friendships are exactly alike.

A friend dies; scenes from our togetherness spring unbidden into mind. At Jack Z.'s funeral I bounced along again in his old car, remembering how he had taken my wife and brand-new daughter and me home from the hospital. At George R.'s funeral I heard again fragments of the many talks we'd had, talks in which he had tried to instill in me some of his convictions about excellence in life. And the astonishing thing we discover, when friends who had winnowed their way securely into our psyches die, is that the old cliché about people who mean something to us never really dying is true. They really *are* there inside ourselves.

The death of a friend forces us—forces some of us—to think deeply about that friendship and about friendships in general. With the special awareness of the grieving, we come upon the paradox that only now, with our friend dead, do we fully realize how meaningful the friendship has been. And we vow that from now on it will be different, from now on we will not take our friendships for granted. But the intensity of our grief fades. We return to everyday life. We resume our other friendships, possibly engender new ones, and only by chance recall, now and again, that promise we'd made to ourselves. That too is part of the process of friendship.

TRENDS

12

Sex and Friendship: How the Sexes Differ

SUCH traits as honesty, trust, and acceptance are important to us regardless of sex, but—judging from the responses to my questionnaire—they are a bit more important to women than to men. Among the college-educated, men clearly place more emphasis on "intellectual stimulation" than do women—and that holds true for men and women still in college, too. Men more than women are apt to be of the same ages, have the same temperaments, and share the same interests as their friends. Single men are more likely than single women to run around exclusively with other singles. Men more than women have educational backgrounds in common with their friends.

Well, all of it is predictable in terms of the cultural stereotypes that were and to a significant extent still are with us. American females have not necessarily been shining examples of emotional openness, but they have certainly shown far more concern about the expressive aspects of relationships—such as trust and acceptance—than American males. Men, far more than women, have been reared to regard brainpower as important. To be free to be more emotional is to be free to be more flexible, so it is no surprise that women show less of a need than men to be evenly matched with their friends in terms of certain background traits.

Many of the friendship studies I examined—at least those that differentiated between the responses of males and females—also reflected the differing cultural impositions that fall upon the two sexes. Dr. Alan Booth of the University of Nebraska scrutinized the friendship patterns of eight hundred adults in two major cities of that state, and found that both working-class and middle-class women had more spontaneous and emotionally richer friendships than did working-class and middle-class men. Dr. Mirra Komarovsky took a comprehensive look at blue-collar marriages and found that six out of every ten wives she interviewed—but only two out of every ten husbands—enjoyed close friendships outside the family. Numerous students of adolescent behavior have noted that as early as the teenage years, girls form more intimate friendships than do boys.

Such conclusions fly in the face of some "conventional wisdom" handed down through the ages: that women are not capable of friendship, that they are certainly not capable of reaching the lofty, noble, magnificent, sublime heights of friendship that men are. "Proof" is that all the legendary friendships of history and literature are between men, which overlooks the fact that only the rare man, as well as the rare woman, is capable of great depth of emotion in any age—and also ignores the fact that the cult of sublime male friendships is based on a derogation of women: all the ladies have a fatal flaw.

"I will not affirm that women have no character, rather they have a new one every day," offered the German poet Heinrich Heine. "To speak the truth, I never yet knew a tolerable woman to be fond of her own sex," was Jonathan Swift's contribution. For D. H. Lawrence it was axiomatic that no woman would ever really commit herself emotionally to a sentimental or intellectual friendship. "A woman depends upon her body far more than she realizes," wrote André Maurois, "she will always give first place to the man she loves physically, and if he insists, will renounce the most perfect friendship for him." Even Simone de Beauvoir, that sensitive delineator of the plight of women, has written, "Women's feelings rarely rise to genuine friendships." But, of course, there is no shortage of women who are far more personal in uttering that conclusion: "I don't like women as much as men" and "I don't take women as seriously as I do men" were comments I heard a number of times from women.

If further justification is needed for the conviction that women are not capable of forging deep friendships with other women, ethnology and anthropology offer rich hunting grounds: wherever friendships are institutionalized, as among the Didinga in Africa and the Tangu in New Guinea, it is usually the men, not the women, who are required to follow the strict guidelines for model friendship—and, anyway, who ever heard of blood sisterhood? Putting the scientific cap on the bottle of diluted female friendships, as it were, is anthropologist Lionel Tiger: his provocative and heavily documented thesis it is that males have a biologically and socially transmitted predisposition, unlike females, to form strong and stable same-sex bonds.

There is truth in all of the foregoing, but it is the kind of half-truth that offers a maddeningly slanted view of things. Given the patriarchal nature of almost every society—that is, their male-based social, religious, literary, and military structures—it is only to be expected that male-male friendships would be the ones celebrated. After all, rulers always fear those they rule and feel safer with their own kind. If men denigrate women—ascribe to them a few fatal flaws—women must come to denigrate themselves; at the very least, not take themselves as seriously as they take men, nor take their own friendships as seriously. If in primitive societies women weren't able to hold positions of power or travel through dangerous countryside as men have been, there was little need for their friendships to be institutionalized and ritualized for the protection of the group. So their friendships have gone unmarked. It is the blood brotherhood, not the quiet, everyday contact, we notice.

As for Tiger, women cannot bond the way men can, he proposes, because their evolutionary history did not demand it. It was men who went hunting and warring by virtue of their superior strength, men who had to keep their small groups together, who had to work cooperatively in order to capture prey and defend themselves. Male bonding meant survival. True, he says, men no longer need to bond in the same way in order to make it through the season and the year, but in time such evolutionary programing serves its own end, becomes its own motivation. So here we are.

Tiger's thesis has tremendous appeal (to men if not to women). Yes, here we are, we men, bound together by a common understanding that predates our existence, predates any notion of recorded history, harks back to the time when we were stalking the wild earth in our little groups, all men (or what then passed for men) brothers or dead. Women don't understand this by now mystical tie that binds us, don't understand the direct evolutionary line that goes from our marauding days to blood brotherhood, all-male bars, all-male sports, male domination of the politico-economic scene. It's not that we're better than you but that we're different; thus there are capacities for bonding, for understanding, between us that you women simply can't fathom. It's through male-male bonding, even today, that the world's *serious* work gets done.

Appealing or not, this male-male bonding theory fails to consider that women too have a need to bond and do bond— sometimes as men do, sometimes at their own pace and in their own way. The picture of primitive men, club in hand, roaming the countryside in search of food is only half the picture, after all; where were the women while the men were off on their adventures? Left behind, together with the children, in the protected base camp, of course. But each female isolated from the other? That seems a little far-fetched. Whatever had to be done—making the fine tools, playing with the children, gathering greens—we can imagine was done cooperatively, each female joining her skill to the other, or, if done alone, done side by side. But there must have been a reason beyond cooperation to bring these early human females together, just as there was to bring the early human males together: they bonded in the service of conquering fear—the fear of being alone, as they must have felt it, the fear of the dark, the fear of nature's cataclysms, of animals, strangers, the unknown. Both sexes must have experienced these fears and bonded for mutual security and support.

If women had no need, or little need, for friendships, women's voluntary organizations would probably lose three fourths of their memberships. In point of fact, such organizations are very popular and the first thing many newcomers in suburban neighborhoods do is to join local clubs and such. An interesting League of Women Voters study (conducted in Los Angeles) illustrates both the friendship needs of women and their ambivalences about the relationship. "Friendships get them into the organization, keep them coming, help to socialize them, and, finally, as one woman put it, get them 'hooked,'" the study states. "The relationship between friendship and commitment is a powerful one because they reinforce each other; those with many friends tend to become committed and once committed develop an ever-expanding circle of friends which, in turn, reinforces the initial commitment."

The study adds that "one of the key factors affecting the friendships among League women was whether or not their husbands liked each other." If there was mutual liking, fine—the women could get together often and be openly close. If the husbands did not care for each other it ended the potential for close friendship among League women even if they liked each other a great deal.

Subordinating their friendships to male preferences is something women have done—have been encouraged to do by the very men who criticize them for being shallow friends—outside organizational frameworks, too. And, as I've already noted, many single women have an "understanding" when they arrange to get together for dinner, or to see a movie, or something: the date stands unless either of them gets a call from a man wanting to take her out that same evening; if she does the date with the girl friend is automatically canceled.

If it is true that numerous women have a need for same-sex friendships, but have been conditioned to keep those friendships subordinate to men's needs and wishes, then the women's liberation movement should be making some difference in these respects. So it is: the movement is having a very direct effect upon some women and an indirect but nevertheless tangible effect upon many others.

"I feel closer to my female friends than I did before," wrote a twenty-one-year-old college student from New Jersey, three years

145

in the movement. "I have actively sought out female companionship and no longer hesitate to talk to a woman at a party if she is
the person who looks most interesting to me. I also feel comfortable about seeing my female friends in many social situations—
movies, restaurants, etc.—places I might previously have felt
uncomfortable in if I didn't 'have' a man." A young aide at a senior
citizens' center in Southern California also touched on this open-
ing-up process: "I've gained the freedom to have closer friendships
with women—I feel freer to express myself honestly with both
women and men friends." And a free-lance editor, sometime
resident of both coasts in recent years, referred to her previous
pattern of devaluing women and elevating men: "I have always
had more male than female friends mainly because I didn't have to
talk babies-and-marriage with the former. And, when I was
younger, I thought men didn't demand as much posturing as
women did. But I had a hard time dating—being with male friends
playing ball, say, and then being expected to treat the date as some
sort of demigod—it was most confusing."

The time-honored middle-class custom of men and women at
dinner parties separating after the repast, the men gathering for
"important" talk, the women for gossip, is even today very much
alive in all but the more cosmopolitan circles. (Few politicians, no
matter how cosmopolitan, deviate from the pattern.) Several
women resentfully remarked on their being shunted off with the
other women when they really wanted to be involved in the
stimulating male talk, and said they had begun to make an issue of
it. But one woman, on the periphery of the women's movement,
was delighted: "I used to mind it but, really, *they're* actually so
boring, *we* have a lot more fun."

In solid lower-middle- and working-class areas, where wom-
en's lib is hardly a household term, women nevertheless are taking
unto themselves "rights" they have not taken on before. In
Quincy, Massachusetts, in Tustin, California, in Cleveland, Ohio,
and in many other locales I heard the same thing: women are now
saying they have the right to an evening out. Women are now
going out for their "night with the girls," just as men traditionally
have taken their "night out with the boys." On one level this is
nothing new. For some time now they have been going out bowling

with the women's team, say, and maybe having beer and pizza afterward. But now a growing number no longer feel they have to structure their socializing around an activity that is understandable and acceptable to men. Instead, these lower-middle- and working-class ladies are going out together to taverns, not to pick up men but to sit and talk.

"Many of these women feel trapped," a social worker in Quincy, Massachusetts, explained; "they feel time is passing them by and they want some fun."

And their husbands? A minority are becoming more flexible in terms of sex roles, the younger men especially—agreeing to take care of the children while their wives socialize with girl friends. But many men, not yet being able to accept the principle of social equality between themselves and their wives, feel threatened. And so marital tension occurs. Family service caseworkers with several units of the Center for Human Services in Cleveland, for instance, say they are seeing an upsurge of applications from husbands whose wives have started spending time with their female friends for evenings out.

Why should women want their evenings out together? For that matter, why should men? We are back to bonding now, but while same-sex associations may have started with the need for security way back in the swampy time of a young and primitive world, being with a friend of the same sex serves a number of psychological needs specifically related to the fact that they *are* of the same sex. The process of same-sex identification, so important and intense during childhood and adolescence, does not really ever stop altogether. Regardless of how old we are, we continue to measure and confirm ourselves to some extent in terms of our roles as men and women. "Even when our identifications are already clearly determined, there is a need for support of them through some association with the same sex" is the way Miriam Weisberg of the Center for Human Services puts it.

There's something else: we are men, we are women—we are separate. Even if one accepts as palpable nonsense the age-old belief that men and women can never really be friends, we may well bring to our cross-sex relationships expectations, angers, or anxieties that act as barriers. Even if we are absolutely, entirely free of such barriers (and is any one of us ever that free?) we are still housed in different bodies, different systems. We hold a great many feelings, experiences, and needs in common—which is why sex-role stereotyping is so arrogant and onerous—but we are different, too.

Yes, different. No matter how sympathetic or empathic we may individually be, men toward women, women toward men, we cannot "know" each other as essentially as men can know men and women can know women. Males can "understand" the capacity for childbirth and to some extent feel it, but not really; males can't really know what it is like to have that kind of body. Males can "understand" the frustrations of a woman who feels trapped by her inability to spend herself creatively because it's taken for granted that she will give her sex-linked roles top priority; males can empathize with her situation, but as to really experiencing what she experiences—well, no, males can't. Similarly, an empathic woman can understand the special accountability that always accrues to the man during the sex act because the penis, unlike the vagina, is a visible symbol of performance success or failure, but she can't truly feel that accountability. She can, if she is sensitive, understand the way men feel trapped by their own competitive needs in a society where the male role, not the female's, is still equated primarily with achievement, but she can't truly experience the emotions involved.

Experience is the crux of it: the histories we build up as men and women are in some ways shared histories but in some ways are not. Those that are not finally always stand between us in male-female relationships. I hardly mean to suggest that there is perfect understanding between men or between women; that would be absurd. I may have a great deal more in common with certain women than I do with certain men. Nevertheless, there are experiences we have in common only with our own sex—special experiences giving rise to special feelings that make the same-sex relationship unique. Automatically, then, when women get together with women and men with men, some things are taken for granted. We know that we know. We assume our shared history. It takes fewer words to communicate; there is less explaining to do. At times the content of our conversations has to be very different, too; not better or worse, superior or inferior, stimulating or boring—but different, because our shared histories point us in those directions. One does not, at the one extreme, have to be sexist, and on the other extreme one does not have to propose a strictly same-sex approach, in order to suggest that sometimes being and talking with a friend of the same sex can be very relaxing.

So men like to get together at times to go hunting or fishing, to settle into Friday-night poker games, to get drunk, to down a couple of beers before going home from work. Don't they enjoy the activity for its own sake? Of course. Isn't getting away from women sometimes a factor? Yes, probably. But the activity they choose is also an excuse for *getting together with men*. Protracted business lunches and meetings, so wasteful and inefficient in terms of accomplishing their stated goals, also serve the same function— a reason men are so resistant to allowing women into the higher executive reaches. Men do not fully understand women—in fact, on the whole probably understand women less than women understand them, because they are less willing to feel, because they don't take the time to feel. So they join—they bond, if you will —in a camaraderie they find only with each other in a comprehensible male society.

And women? Women join together for the same purposes (though often with less energy) in PTAs and volunteer organizations, at bridge parties where there may well be more talk than bridge, on bowling leagues, arts-crafts sessions and the like. Consciousness-raising groups are so popular with many women now not only because it gives them a chance to talk about feelings and attitudes they may have long kept suppressed but also because the atmosphere is one that in general, at least for the duration of each session, engenders a feeling that really is akin to "sisterhood."

Enfin, both sexes need same-sex as well as cross-sex outlets— easily accessible places where, if they so wish, they can relax with others of their sexual kind. Women's movement leaders have campaigned, somewhat successfully, for the abolition of all-male bars, dining rooms, and other such sex-segregated facilities. As a reaction to discrimination—to the reality of the economic, political, and other power that men hold over women, it is a plausible move. It symbolizes and particularizes the anger that women for so long held in check, or did not know they had, at being shut out of important spheres of life. But if the needs of both sexes are considered apart from tactics and emotion, a diversity of facilities would be helpful, where men and women could be together or apart, in accordance with their inclination of the moment.

If a sense of discovery now pervades the friendships of women, or of some women, in the United States, a sense of ambiguity and paradox has usually pervaded the friendships of American males. Men have always been in a rather untenable position with respect to the reaching out for friends. Like women they have, to greater or lesser degree, that "appetite for contact." But they have also inherited a host of cultural biases and myths about themselves— one being that they are less emotional than women, another being that their friendships are "truer" than those of women. This contradiction has made things topsy-turvy for men in terms of friendship: if we are to believe the stereotype, men's friendships are really more solid and emotionally steadfast—but women are the ones who have the greater leeway in showing affection to same-sex friends. Because they have subscribed to rigid sex-role stereo-typing, men have allowed themselves precious few options on the whole—two, in fact. Either keep a proper distance from your friends or be considered suspect (and suspect yourself) of homosexuality. Under these circumstances, any time a man feels affectionate toward a male friend, feels he needs a male friend, he must question his masculinity.

I am obviously overstating the case. Firstly, the greater freedom American women have in this respect is relative. A number of foreign women, fairly new arrivals to the United States, told me how much more expressive women are in their homelands. A Greek girl, for instance, told of walking a Greek-American friend to her apartment house and then kissing her on the cheek goodbye; the Greek-American girl blushed and said, "Don't do that again on the street. They'll think we're lesbians." An American woman told of her experiences with an African woman who was staying with her: "She was so close and expressive, she'd touch. She was uninhibited about that, but I wasn't. But after a while I learned to relax and enjoy it—it's pleasant, we miss a lot."

I am also overstating the case because just as American women are hardly shining examples of uninhibited friends, so American men are not cardboard figures mechanically adhering to those constricting stereotypes. All males are influenced by them, but how and to what degree depends on the particular man. It is idiosyncratic. There are men who will admit to a dependency upon friends—while looking askance at the Turkish custom of men walking hand in hand. There are men who can easily throw an arm around a friend—but insist with all their might that they are completely self-sufficient. There are men who will show their friends all kinds of little kindnesses—tokens of affection—while simultaneously masking that affection with a kind of good-natured banter.

Thus, however they manifest themselves, those stereotypes have a constant effect on male-male friendships. For many males it is as if, in conducting their friendships, they have to be constantly poised to flee any implication of homosexuality. The English sociologist Geoffrey Gorer pinpoints an example of this in discussing roommate or "buddy" relationships of great intensity: the closer the tie between the two men, the more intent they are likely to be on chasing girls. Maybe they like those girls, maybe they don't. But in chasing them they ward off the threat of anything homosexual possibly existing in the relationship.

Sports is one of the few areas where men have managed to ritualize affection and thereby make it acceptable: locker-room hijinks, swats across the bottom, bear hugs—such ritualized touching transforms acts that would be considered sexually provocative in other settings into exemplary masculine behavior. Drinking can do it, too, in the proper (masculine) settings: when I interviewed American Legion and Veterans of Foreign Wars veterans it was always at their respective posts, and almost always in the bar or lounge; and almost always after drinking for a few hours some of the men would become obviously affectionate with each other, as is only natural since they were close friends and since the conversation revolved around friendship. But it was obvious that this was a spontaneity they would not show without being high.

Freud had very little to say about friendship. One of the few things he did say was that friendship is "aim-inhibited sexuality" which all the clinicians take to mean homosexuality. To extrapolate along Freudian lines, then: having been brought up by two parents, male and female, we have homosexual as well as heterosexual "pulls" to our natures, and straight men and women can sublimate their homosexual pulls in nonsexual, same-sex friendships. Following this line of clinical reasoning further, persons who have somewhat strong homosexual leanings but do not wish to succumb to them use their same-sex friendships as a "corrective" measure without necessarily (or even usually) being aware of it. This is especially the case with men because society doesn't allow them to be as overtly affectionate with their own sex as women are allowed to be with theirs. Thus two men playing golf or handball every Saturday afternoon may have a "romantic" relationship without either of them ever knowing that it is so.

This equation, however, is not all that helpful. If we all have homosexual pulls and most of us defend ourselves against them— desexualize them—by our same-sex friendships, then the only thing left to say is, so what? But in fact the definition is absurdly simplistic; as the previous chapters have shown, a complex of phylogenetic, sociological, and psychological considerations are at work in our friendship formations. To say that friendship is nothing but sublimated homosexuality is akin to saying that the human body is three-fourths water; it omits some essentials.

Part of the problem is not Freud's; it is ours. We tend to oversexualize everything, jump over mountains of concerns and feelings and resistances to the conclusion that if there is an erotic element to anything it immediately means "wanting to go to bed with." When we feel close to someone—child, parent, friend, or lover—we also have the natural inclination (one we share with the other animals) to translate those feelings of closeness into physical terms. Words, no matter how eloquent, are not enough. Looks, no matter how soulful, are not enough. We are physical as well as intellectual beings. So we have the urge, sometimes, to translate our warm and tender feelings into action. As zoologist Desmond Morris says, "The ability that physical feelings have to transmit emotional feelings is truly astonishing." But when we oversexualize such physical expressions we cannot tolerate whatever libidinous content they may have. It becomes too scary, for the jump is made (in our imagination) from feeling to bedding down.

Some of this goes on in every society, for every society has its taboos which serve to regulate the sexual behavior of its members. But we carry things to an extreme. American men who think nothing of petting a dog because they're fond of it (haven't they heard of bestiality?) would never dream of embracing a friend they are fond of. Russian men, on the other hand, have bear-hugged and cheek-kissed each other for centuries without worrying about their masculinity. Russian men cheek-kiss their friends but American men immediately wonder if they are homosexuals if they even so much as have the fleeting impulse. At colleges and universities, psychiatrists and counselors report that some students come seeking professional advice about this issue: they want to know if something is the matter with them because they feel affectionate toward close friends or roommates. The same concern often crops up when men get together in male consciousness-raising groups, of which there are some three hundred scattered around the United States.

That men—that some men—can question themselves about such things today is a very encouraging sign. Sexologists and sociologists debate just how revolutionary the sexual revolution really is; some feel that things have really not changed that much, but that they have simply surfaced more. Be that as it may, there should be no question about how much loosening up has been going on in terms of thought, speech, and fantasy. The women's movement and the gay liberation movement, too, are forcing men to consider their lives and roles as males; even men who do not have the slightest direct contact with such movements are subtly influenced by them, if only (it is really not "only") to ask themselves questions about their roles as men that they wouldn't have asked themselves before.

So one notices changes: several interviewees, for instance,

reported on the college reunions they had recently attended. Here they were, coming together again after ten years, fifteen years, twenty years, with men they had been buddies with way back then when the world was shiny and the future unspoiled by reality. In the poignancy of the moment these balding, paunchy middle-aged men with their matronly wives were happy as kids to see each other again, and some, carried away by their feelings, hugged and kissed each other. They were really not "carried away" except in the sense of hurdling long-held inhibitions. They were really acting in ways appropriate to the emotion they felt.

And a few men also told me little stories of their own unfolding, their personal discovery that being emotional with friends, being intimate with friends, being physical with friends, can have a far different connotation than they imagined. Steve, a young social worker, is one such. He had recently become friendly with a new group of men, he said, and as they engaged in a bull session a few nights earlier one of the men said, "You know, Steve, you're really a beautiful person." For Steve it was an extraordinary moment. "I might have heard something like that from a woman, but never from my old friends," he told me. "With my closest friend there's always a lot of kidding around and holding each other off—like, if he had a good time and wants to see me again soon he'll say, 'Don't call me, I'll call you.' It was really nice having another man saying how he really felt."

Max is another example. He was away on a business trip when his closest friend's daughter was being married; wanting to be there, both for himself and for his friend, he flew back just for the wedding day, departing again late that night. "When we said goodbye," Max related, "my friend and I shook hands, as we always do. It had been a warm, wonderful day, a really beautiful wedding, and I told him so. I could see something in his face— something about how glad he was I'd made it back for the wedding. Well, it was a strange moment because here were two friends, really telling each other how much caring there was between them, and shaking hands seemed so—well, nothing, empty. And then I did something I'd never done before in my life, but it just seemed so natural. I hugged him and then, in front of our wives and kids and God and everybody I kissed him. You know what he did? Grinned at me, and said, 'You son of a bitch, *I* wanted to do that!' "

Max said he has not, since then, made a pastime of kissing men —yet the experience had left him feeling a little bemused and very much pleased with himself, as though "it had been a test of some kind and I passed it beautifully."

What he probably meant was that he could do something that went against all his concepts of masculinity and still not lose his sense of himself as a man—that, if you will, he could do something "homosexual" without succumbing or wanting to succumb to homosexuality. If the liberating forces at work in American society continue as they have, many more men will discover this. Will discover that they have more power and control over their sex lives than they thought possible, which will allow them to be freer.

But for some other men won't one step lead to another, from male-male affection to male-male sexual experimentation, from experimentation to an exclusively homosexual style of life? The answer for some persons is—of course. Back in 1970, already, a Chicago-based men's liberation group issued a manifesto that read in part, "We have met with our brothers from Gay Liberation and have begun to deal with the whole problem in our heads concerning homosexuality and our fear toward men sharing sex with other men, or women sharing sex with other women. None of us feels that we have come close to completing this, but the problems are out in the open and we feel that together we can deal with our deepest fears."

Right along, of course, men have been swinging this way and that, as have women. Hypocrisy aside, we have always been a sexually pluralistic society; this is simply more on the surface now, alternatives are more readily acknowledged. The advantage of barriers falling is that it does allow people—men *and* women—to assume more direct, straighforward control over their sexual lives —at least, since we are all guided by hidden as well as conscious motivations, over those desires and impulses we recognize and, hopefully, understand. Societally and individually, we erect our conventions (our safety devices) as we need them, and begin to dismantle them as we find them less useful. As anthropologist Margaret Mead has said, more varied sexual behavior can be tolerated when procreation is no longer the focus of sex. It probably is safe to assume that bisexual play and homosexuality will be on the upswing—without, however, any danger of the species dying out.

It would be stretching the imagination, though, to suggest that people who engage in sex play with their same-sex friends are so overcome with affection that this is the only way they can express it. That happens, but lots of other things happen, too. The language of sex is never—well, rarely—so uncomplicated; how we use sex or do not use sex is indicative of our personalities as a whole. Curiosity, hostility, boredom, fear, impulsiveness, feelings about emotional commitment—these and a host of other factors, singly or compounded, influence our sexual choices and behaviors. The women's movement and the way it has become instrumental in crystallizing in many women the feeling of being trapped and victimized by men is a case in point. A woman active in the movement as writer and interpreter explained, "If you're no longer willing to tolerate certain kinds of behavior on the part of men that you tolerated before, you're drawing away from many males that you once knew. Where can you go from there? You have only one sex left, and that's your own. And with some women, coming to the point where they're able to like other women and love other women, the next step is physical love."

"Liberation movements" such as the women's and the gay activists' are liberating to many people not directly involved with them in that they make it permissible to express thoughts and possible to consider choices that were hitherto taboo. Among some of the chic women in New York City, Los Angeles, and a few other cosmopolitan cities, bisexuality is now the "in" thing if not in deed then in fantasy; I encountered a number of middle-class wives who admitted they had been flirting with the idea, fantasizing a bit with their most trusted female friends. But it is not affection or love for their female friends that has suddenly overcome them—those trusted friends, friends who think as they do, allow them to talk about the untalkable. And if they do experiment with women it is probably those close friends they will experiment with—again, not because they are so moved by the friendship but because the environment is safe. One lady candidly said, "Look, we're all in our thirties, all married and mothers of young children—and we're all a little disillusioned with our lives. Our husbands are—well, just not that exciting any more. We've had our affairs and they haven't exactly set our world on fire. So what do bored and jaded ladies do? They start thinking of other ways to spice their lives. . . ."

13

Sex and Friendship: Platonic Realities

"*THE* women's movement," I was to hear again and again from women active in the movement, "is enabling women to draw closer to each other, making friendships genuinely possible. But the movement is raising havoc with friendships *between* the sexes."

Of that conclusion, one could fairly ask, *what* friendships? When women and men see each other in stereotypical roles, as historically has been the case to now, only expectations based on "You're a man" and "You're a woman" are easily possible. Every encounter between a woman and a man then becomes heavy with unspoken demands: confirm that I'm desirable, acknowledge my virility, my orgasmic capacity, prove to me that I'm a sexual being —that's your role, that's your job. Such expectations make true cross-sex friendships difficult if not impossible to achieve. The position of women as not quite the equal of men is hardly a congenial setting for the establishment of such friendships. In fact, under the circumstances the very idea of platonic friendships is enough to send one into a spasm of cynicism; witness Maurois and Proust as typical examples: platonic friendships, they said, can only exist when the man is a lovesick mouse trailing after a woman who cares nothing for him but it amuses her to have him around. The underlying assumption: a real man, a man with a man's penis, will "score"; if he is unable to, fate has slipped him a Mickey—he is a mouse.

But now the stereotypes are being questioned and in some cases breaking down a bit; more and more women are working at better jobs in closer contact with men; in some fields (for instance, in the academic community), colleague relationships are beginning to develop between females and males—so anything is possible for us, even platonic friendships. In fact, all the signs point to a growing number of such friendships in the years ahead. That, in turn, may result in increasing amounts of conflict, especially among married people and those in marriage-type relationships. The subject deserves a closer look.

However, let us define our terms. A friendship without sex is not a sexless friendship. We all have our sexual drives, thoughts, fantasies, and concerns. Our sexual selves are part of our total selves—something that assumes even sharper significance in a society that focuses so much on the sexual side of life as ours does. We are never allowed to forget sex. Sexual elements, then, are always present in a platonic friendship—either overtly, on the level of "I find this person attractive," or on the level of testing oneself, one's desirability, against the other, or on the level of enjoyment at being considered attractive by one's platonic friend. Such things may occur only as nuances—on the subtlest, most indirect and delicate of levels—but they occur. Even if it is clearly understood that sexual relations are completely outside the framework of the relationship—for instance, some women told me they can only really relax completely in the company of men who are homosexual men—sex enters into the relationship paradoxically: by the very awareness on the part of one or both of how unself-consciously they can relate to each other.

If all this is so, does it mean a platonic friendship is impossible? Not unless one is so much of a purist as to insist that only a relationship totally devoid of *any* erotic element is really platonic— but then one may be less purist than puritanical. Even Webster's Third New International Dictionary does not describe platonic love as being devoid of any nuance of sex, merely as having the sexual aspect so suppressed or sublimated as to make one believe it is absent. An unmarried woman, a nurse deeply involved in church work, made it evident how she had worked out the problem for herself: "I doubt that such a thing exists as a completely platonic friendship," she wrote. "I'm celibate (like a nun, only I'm not a nun) and my platonic friends are also celibate. There is no sexual activity but there are varying degrees of attraction. This energy is channeled away from the physical into what could perhaps be called 'creative energy.'"

(There is also a tangential view of platonic relationships, that they are platonic even when the friends do occasionally engage in sexual relations—the rationale being that the focus is on the friendship, not the sex. Wonderful friendships marked by infrequent but enjoyable sexual breaks certainly do occur—sometimes even between former spouses or lovers—but to call them platonic is to make a specific word fit an idiosyncratic definition, at which point the word loses its meaning.)

It can hardly be said that presently we in America are flocking to establish platonic friendships, or that many of those of us who do—whether married or single—rest easy in these relationships. Not surprisingly, platonic friendships are especially tentative when one or both of the friends are married. Of course, every husband and wife involved in a nonsexual friendship with another husband and wife are perforce involved in platonic friendships with the cross-sex spouses of the other pair (unless they get into swapping or unilateral affairs, in which case the relationship becomes something else). On the whole, this kind of platonic friendship is taken for granted and not much talked about—often not even considered platonic, though husbands and wives sometimes do have their fantasies and sometimes do kid each other about being attracted to a friend. But the attraction, unless it grows into something else, is usually low-key, diffuse because four people are interacting; also society, by sanctioning this kind of cross-sex relationship, effectively helps downplay the erotic elements, or at least makes it easier to pretend nothing is going on.

As for two opposite-sex friends having an exclusive relationship even though one or both are married—well, despite the popularity of "open marriage" viewpoints, most of the married people I spoke with were distinctly uneasy about the whole idea: too tempting, won't work, only starts something innocent that becomes something else—these were the prevailing attitudes by far. Even many of the "liberated" marrieds either talked in terms of infidelity—that it's okay in marriage, thereby denying the possibility of platonic relationships—or of cross-sex friendships restricted to narrow and specific ways in which the two friends can be together without threatening the marriage: you can have lunch with a cross-sex friend, for example, but you can't go out for a drink after work or in the evening; too disturbing for the marriage partner left behind.

I asked twenty-five family-service agencies, representing a fair geographical cross section of the country, to offer their views on the feasibility and advisability of married persons maintaining cross-sex frienships. By and large, family-service workers do not hold far-out sexual views and are reasonably in touch with prevailing community standards and expectations. Five agencies flatly rejected the possibility of cross-sex friendship in marriage: because they only create tensions; because even if they don't lead to romances they create hurt feelings on the part of the spouses excluded from the friendships because others of their sex are fulfilling some of their mates' needs. In effect, husband and wife must "possess" each other, be everything to each other. As for the rest of the agencies, they said that if the marriage is strong and the two partners mature platonic friendships are fine—are constructive, even, because they help the people involved understand the opposite sex better. But then they added so many caveats that it became quite evident they do not see many people in their areas having marriages that strong or being that mature.

Among the interviewees who answered my questionnaire, singles—and younger singles at that—represented the largest group reporting platonic friends. Not infrequently friendships which started with sexual intent but did not turn out that way became solid friendships. Some were the aftermath of love affairs —"You've slept together and that's over with and you will have a real warm feeling toward each other," is the way a librarian in New York City put it. "You get to the point where you're looking at a lot of other people but you still like this one, right? So you matter-of-factly know that's that, but it doesn't stop you from being friends. You can enjoy each other much more casually when the sex thing is no longer there, and you don't have to worry about performance," is the way an antiques dealer in Los Angeles, a homosexual male, put it. Several male students at Georgetown University in Washington, D.C., talked about "trying to conquer a girl and then finding out you're not compatible that way but she's a real nice chick, and then you become friends," as one student said, or "using a girl to get to another girl you're really after, but then finding out what a good friend the girl being used is," as another student said, "so you can start out manipulatively and end up as something real."

All of the singles involved in platonic friendships had good things to say about those kinds of friendships: you don't have to "perform" as you do in other male-female relationships where the sexual element is more overtly present, you don't have to make decisions pro or con about having sex, you learn more about the "male" and "female" points of view, you get a more objective response with regard to certain issues than you can from boy friends or girl friends one is romantically involved with, you can talk about problems you're having with boy friends and girl friends.

But many also said how hard it was to make such friendships and to keep them from becoming physical, or having the physical aspects play an inhibiting role. A number of college students living in coed dorms told of how nice and relaxing, how conducive to platonic friendships, it was to be men and women living naturally together, padding around in bathrobes, waiting in line for the same shower, telling each other one's problems. But then the real world impinges—that part of the world that equates a male-female pair with sex and sets up sexualized performance requirements for such pairs; thus eventually one of the pair is apt to wonder, "Why am I only a sister to him?" or, "Why does he treat me like a brother—am I so unappealing?" I heard the same kind of thing from outside the campus—actually, more often about men than about women: "We were such good friends, I even told him about my more romantic relationships," said a woman, thirty, relating a fairly typical experience, "but after a few months he asked me to sleep with him—if I did it with other men, why not him? I was shocked; I knew it wasn't me he wanted, but his masculinity was on the line. . . . We said goodbye."

Consistency is not one of the most pronounced of human characteristics; some singles talked about how valuable their platonic friendships were, but then said that they had little time for them because they were so busy dating romantically or sexually. "It's hard to get the thing together; you're not meeting each other's sexual needs," said an office manager, who had just gotten through recounting her rich platonic relationships with two men, one straight, the other homosexual.

Where I found platonic friendships to be most successful is on the teenage level. Despite the heavy emphasis in both the popular and the professional literature on teenage sex, the fact is that everywhere I went, talking to teenagers and to qualified observers of the teenage scene, I heard that what is new and different about teenage friendship is the growing incidence of nonsexual, nonromantic friendships between adolescent boys and girls. In some cases they are even "best friends."

Of course, this is a reaction to the intense peer-group pressure to perform sexually; platonic friendships make it possible for boys and girls to be together without having to perform, yet also give each sex, during this impressionable and eager age, a chance to learn something about the other—about how the other thinks and behaves. Teenagers involved in platonic friendships often get impatient with scoffing parents—parents who suspect that something sexual is going on even when their sons and daughters righteously insist, "We're just *friends.*" Both are correct: the relationship is sexual in that both the boy and the girl are testing their emerging maleness and femaleness against each other, albeit in a "safe" environment; the relationship is not sexual in the sense the parents mean because, even though they might not conceive it to be possible, nothing physical is going on.

What is going on in such circumstances is that the boys and girls involved in platonic relationships are learning social skills that will stand them in good stead both in their sexual and nonsexual relations with the opposite sex. It is a beneficent circle these teenagers are caught in: the sexual revolution has taken a lot of the mystery out of sex, so now boys and girls can approach each other less tentatively, less fearfully, more openly; associating with each other further reduces the mystery that has always been attached to the opposite sex; both can see, with a clarity not given to people who don't have or avoid the opportunity, that both sexes are human—and vulnerable.

Platonic friendships at whatever age are not made in heaven; their patterns are learned right here on earth, subject to the cultural pressures of the time. Today's teenagers, newly starting this learning process, and starting it so young, may—just may—as adults be able to approach each other more easily, freely, casually, and acceptingly in both their sexual and nonsexual relationships than most adults now seem able to do. But that depends on how widespread the phenomenon will become and, therefore, on how much it will influence a change in the prevailing psychosexual patterns that mark our culture.

14

The Myths of Friendship

MORE than just a word with a couple of dictionary definitions, "friendship" is the embodiment of ideas about the way people should behave in engaging in a certain facet of human interaction. Each culture has its own notions about this. Many, both primitive and modern, idealize the friendship tie—that is, they set up standards of behavior that are very nearly impossible to carry out. So it is for us: "friendship" embodies a rich legacy of idealized thought, beginning with, but hardly restricted to, the Greeks.

To take seriously all of the prescriptions for friendship handed down to us throughout the ages is to live a life of absolute perfection—at least within the context of friendship. We should love our friends only for what they are, not for what we can get out of them. Since friendship—"perfect" friendship, at any rate—is between two persons who are equally good, we must wish only good for each other and desire only to bring out the best in each other.

Being a "coincidence of free souls," as Santayana put it, friends are never jealous of each other, never attempt to lord it over each other, never become possessive with each other. Regardless of how trying or troubling a situation may be, we continue to help our friends; we stick with them through thick and thin. We must never lie to our friends, though it is better to remain silent than to sting them with criticism—"I am so much and so exclusively the friend of my friend's virtue that I am compelled to be silent for the most part, because his vice is present. I am made dumb by this third party," is the way Thoreau elegantly put it. In friendship, finally, we are utterly selfless, finding our joys in our friends' successes, our sorrows in our friends' misfortunes—"our constant purpose," to quote a nineteenth-century American writer on the subject, H. C. Trumbull, "is the doing and enduring for the friend."

Nobody can quarrel with standards of conduct that ennoble our relationships with each other—except when those standards are presented in such a way as to suggest that anything less means a failed friendship or a failed friend, and that is exactly how they have been presented. Not willing to acknowledge our human failings as well as virtues, not willing to accept the fact that the best we can do is try, the idealists pave the way for an inevitable panic of disillusionment because nobody can live up to their expectations. So it was, for example, that Aristotle finally burst forth with a poignant "O my friends, there is no friend" and a bitter David Hume, the eighteenth-century Scottish philosopher, wrote, "The difficulty is not so great to die for a friend, as to find a friend worth dying for." The friendship has to measure up, or the friendship is second-rate. Black and white.

I hardly mean to suggest that contemporary Americans are so naive or innocent as to seriously believe we can relate to each other with all traces of jealousy, self-interest, possessiveness, competitiveness, and other less ennobling elements of character forever absent. Nor did a single interviewee convey the impression that complete devotion to the friendship, as proposed by the idealists, was expected. And yet—this is so difficult to quantify—perhaps a third of the people I talked with showed some degree of disillusionment with their friendships or with the concept of friendship in general. Not that it was always very strong—sometimes there was just a hint of disenchantment. They usually did not talk about any specific friend having let them down; that feeling of disillusionment was vaguer, more diffuse. As if they expected something more from friendship, something people may have had in the past . . . . But what? That often remained unclear. So I began to wonder about the mythologizing of the friendship tie and of the effect this has had. We do not rationally believe the myths, perhaps; but—well, maybe we don't altogether disbelieve them, either. *Friendship*: the power of the word.

Among my interviewees were numerous immigrants, of course, and Americans who have been exposed to customs in foreign lands; from some of them I heard the theme that friendships are deeper, closer, more meaningful in those countries than they are at home. I talked at length with more than three dozen foreigners—many of them foreign students—residing in the United States. A clear majority responded to questions about their friendships with Americans along the lines of "You let us down." Whether they came from France or Ceylon or Tunisia or Jamaica or Ethiopia or other disparate corners of the world, their themes were the same: we met you in our home countries, and you were so open and warm and friendly, so we came to your land expecting to find you the same—but you let us down. You are too preoccupied with yourselves, too concerned with making money or achieving this or that to take the time to develop friendships—you let us down. We always took the time to chat, and we were in each other's houses when you were in our homelands, but now you have so little time to talk and we are not invited in—you let us down. We interpret your curiosity and concern about us, when you show it, as genuine testimony to our friendship, but when we need help, where are you? You aren't around—you let us down.

Are we really so superficial or is this a classic case of distorted impressions enhanced by cultural differences? The issue is important, for in some respects it gets to the heart of our American way of friendship, its values, and its shortcomings. To begin with, this is a situation ready-made for misunderstanding: here's the American abroad, out of his accustomed routine, far less hurried than at home, feeling displaced and therefore more needful of friendship, giving the impression of relaxed friendliness. It is a genuine reflection of his feelings then and there, and it is assumed by those who observe him that this is what he is always like. Imbued with this image of the American, the foreigner comes to the United States, himself now displaced and needing friends, expecting Americans to conform to his image of them but seeing them only in their quickened, typically American pace, busily caught up in their day-to-day routines. The contrast is sharp, the disillusionment painful; the foreigner stands ready to be harder on friendships in America and kinder on friendships in his homeland than either might deserve. Cultural shock is not the handmaiden of objectivity.

All kinds of cultural differences, reflecting different societal or class styles and goals, make their impact on friendship. French bourgeois children are strictly supervised in terms of the friends they are allowed to make; they learn both that the family comes first and that one's devotion is to the family and a very tight circle of well-established friends. By contrast, we grow up learning that there need not be a contradiction between loose family ties and strong loyalty to friends. In India, where cross-sex adolescent dating is frowned upon, intense same-sex friendships last through the teenage years and persist into adulthood, even after marriage. We dilute the intensity of our adolescent same-sex friendships the moment we begin seriously to date, and from then on there is always a competition between romance and friendship, most of us wishing to invest more in the romantic attachments. Fraternity systems in England, Holland, and elsewhere have created a strong all-male upper-class subculture whose members remain lifelong friends and derive lifelong social, business, and political benefits. Stratified as we are, it is nevertheless more difficult for such networks to remain exclusive in the United States, and many of us who could attempt it prefer more diversity in our social relationships.

Often confusing to other people, and sometimes to ourselves as well, is the way we style our friendships. In contrast to those in many other countries, ours are less structured, less formalized, more spontaneous and easygoing. Like everybody else we have our expectations of what the friendship role is like, but those expectations are far more subject to our individual idiosyncrasies, much less rooted in formal (or "understood") rules and regulations. Our pace of life *is* fast (though getting faster in most other countries, too), we *are* into many things, and if at times we simply say hello to friends and move on, without inquiring about the babies and the grandparents and the begonia trees, everybody—well, almost everybody—understands. Our mobility, geographical and across class lines, makes us much less assured that our current friends will be our friends tomorrow—in distinct contrast to many nations, such as Germany, where friendships are seen as irretrievably binding.

Finally, we are victims of our own friendliness: too quick to use the world "friend" when all we mean is, "You're somebody pleasant to be with"—having nothing to do with commitment. *We* know what we mean, and though it could fairly be said that the word "friend" becomes debased when used so casually, we don't take it that seriously. Not, at any rate, in that specific context. Our minds make automatic distinctions between using "friend" in a real relationship sense, and hearing ourselves referred to as "friend" by people who met us a scant half hour before. Others, accustomed to clear differentiation between friends and acquaint-ances, and whose language may even have words to denote the differing degrees of friendship, are confused. Their confusion is compounded by our lack of reticence and casual use of people's first names. What we see as friendliness they see as overtures to friendship—or as a sign that we are incapable of forming serious friendships. The way is left open for lots of misinterpretation.

Nowhere is there a "perfect" style of friendship. There are always gains and losses. Reserve makes possible slow and pre-sumably lasting friendships—at a serious cost to spontaneity. To feel assured that childhood friends will be friends throughout adulthood brings security—but at the price of remaining settled, forsaking growth and advancement, and possibly encouraging tedium. To retain in adulthood the luminous intensity of adolescent friendship means restricting the depth of marital or marriagelike relationships. In our friendships we have looseness and spontanei-ty, a lack of restrictiveness (especially in the middle class)—but our friendships are more empirical, but also more tentative.

That our friendships are more empirical also makes it seem as though we "use" our friends in the way people elsewhere do not. In fact, we are often accused of establishing our friendships on the basis of practical rather than emotional considerations, and quite a few of my interviewees were clearly resistant to the notion of friends "using" friends.

There certainly is a way of crassly using people to one's own advantage and, while that kind of thing goes on everywhere, logic alone would dictate that the more materialistic and achievement-oriented the culture, the higher the incidence of such exploitation. In that sense we stand indicted. On the other hand, much of what seems like exploitation really is not. Men do not join Kiwanis to make friends but to gain business advantages; this is clearly understood and if they develop friendly feelings for each other in the process, so much the better; and if friendships develop in the sense that the people involved enjoy their association, better still. When people pretend to like other people in order to gain certain advantages, cultivating these relationships strictly to that end, it is exploitation. But even then things are not always so clear-cut. There are enough gullible persons around, God knows, but there are also lots of people who allow themselves to be fooled—who enjoy being exploited, no matter how much they may protest about it later on. The politician who glad-hands everyone around is an example. Unless he and I have other things going for us I will not be impressed by his show of friendship; I know he needs my vote and/or my services. But I'm not so easily fooled, I think; if I permit myself to be seduced by that friendly manner of his I'm not really that innocent a victim: surely I'm getting something out of the transaction—the enjoyment of knowing an "important" person, feeling more important myself for knowing him, reckoning that someday he'll be good for a favor. . . . Which of us is exploiting the other? Not all friendships need to be made in heaven.

It simplifies things to categorize people's behavior, but categories are no reflection of real life with all its subtleties and nuances. Many social scientists have approached the study of friendships in primitive societies categorically; they have noted that there are "instrumental" friendships—those that lead to a particular goal— and "affective" friendships—those established for the emotional content involved. Anthropologist Robert Paine persuasively disagrees, noting that both types "are found in combination," making it "quite misleading to distinguish kinds of friendships on the basis of one or another of the attributes." A particular friendship pattern may be highly institutionalized, put into effect to accomplish some very specific societal goals. Yet it can be of the highest moral order and also give the friends involved an opportunity for emotional exchanges.

In our own world business friendships are usually seen as highly utilitarian, if not outrightly exploitative. But relationships cannot always be so rigorously defined. A bunch of students getting their masters at the Harvard Business School make friends with each other. Presumably most will be influential in the business world someday and therefore good people to know. Do they become friends with each other because of the advantages that may—probably will—someday accrue as a result of these relationships? Or are students drawn to each other on the basis of mutual liking? More to the point, glaring instances of exploitation and manipulation excepted, can the two motivations really be separated?

Or take a pharmaceutical salesman, thirty years on the job. For thirty years he plays golf with every druggist, distributor, and jobber in his territory, has dinner with them and their families, involves himself in their lives and them in his. Well, how much of his interest in them is "real" and how much prompted by commercial considerations? But then he retires and spends the next fifteen years kibbitzing around with the very same people. Sure, his relationship with them had a very strong utilitarian element to it when he was selling—but it obviously satisfied some other needs, too.

Workers in factories and large offices often develop group friendships that amount to cliques. Of course they like each other or they would not have banded together in the particular constellations that come to be—but they "use" each other, too: as conduits for work-related gossip; for mutual support; to keep from feeling too powerless, too dominated, by the shop or office brass.

All of us, whatever kinds of friendships we are involved in, "use" each other. Previous chapters pointed out the myriad ways this process goes on: to gain emotional rewards, to achieve connectedness with the world, to confirm our values, to confirm our worth, to sublimate aggression, to be strengthened by friends' strengths, and more. Two friends who engage in animated discussion that sparks ideas "use" each other to stimulate a rush of creative impulse. The act of giving pleasure to or helping a friend brings us genuine pleasure in return. I don't mean to suggest that we calculatingly give pleasure in order to receive it—the act of giving flows naturally out of the relationship—but if giving weren't pleasurable it wouldn't be as popular as it is.

To some degree all friendships are symbiotic. All friendships are rooted in reciprocity—certainly not on a strict I-do-something-for-you-so-you-do-something-for-me basis, but over the breadth of the relationship. Outsiders might see a particular relationship in terms of one friend exploiting the other. But that is irrelevant to what goes on between the friends themselves; each may be getting just what he or she wants out of their tie. As A. W. Gouldner points out in a classic paper on the subject, reciprocity plays a "stabilizing role in human relations"—and that includes the most intimate.

But what if this reciprocity breaks down? What if one of the friends feels dissatisfied after a time—feels his own needs are not being met, or the other's needs are being met far more than his own? At that point what was symmetry in the relationship becomes asymmetry. When we are in asymmetrical relationships we are bothered, we cannot sustain our role in the friendship very long without some kind of reaction. We may turn inward, consciously or not stoking the fires of resentment. We may lash out in anger. The woman whose own psychic strength is being depleted in the process of helping a close friend who is in constant emotional turmoil begins to withdraw. The man who no longer feels served at either position of a fixed dominance-submission tie attempts to shift the balance of the relationship and, failing that, ends the friendship in some way.

I think we have to reexamine the concept of "old friends." In the idealization of friendship the long-lasting—no, the lifetime—relationship is the only truly worthy one; everything else falls short of the mark. No question but that old friends fill a very special place in our lives. The history between us is more than just a bunch of shared experiences spread over a certain amount of time. More, even, than the emotional investment we have in each other—though that, of course, is very important, too. Old friends,

friends stretching back over time, are a link between the persons we were and the persons we are; they give continuity to our lives; they anchor us, in some curious way, to the reality of our pasts, thereby confirming us more securely in the reality of the present.

Everyone I interviewed—everyone—could refer to old friends in their lives. They did not necessarily see those old friends very often —but there they were, felt and alive. Some of these relationships were truly long-standing: like the sixty-two-year-old woman whose oldest friend, back in her home town, she had known for sixty-two years, and whom she saw on annual visits home; like the sixty-nine-year-old man who had known his oldest friend for forty-eight years—they had met as parishioners in the same church—and whom he sees every few years. There is the group of six friends who grew up together on the streets of Brooklyn; went into the service where they scattered; came home; married; went into different occupations, some prospering more than others; all moving away finally, some to Manhattan, some to the suburbs. . . . A familiar story with a novel end: for the past twenty years all six friends have been meeting every Wednesday night in restaurants accessible to all, in order to be together and talk. They don't talk about anything special, not about personal matters—yet they feel tremendously fond and supportive of each other. Having known each other for almost their whole lives, they keep fond childhood memories alive by their remarkable weekly get-togethers.

Vital as old friends are in our lives, though, we have to ask ourselves whether they are the only measure by which we can judge the richness of our relationships. The ideal of the lifetime friend was born when men pursued the art of friendship with more vigor than they pursued the art of marriage. It has endured in a stabler but necessarily more limiting time than ours—when people could reasonably count on living in the same kinds of neighborhoods, working at the same kinds of jobs, pursuing the same interests, throughout their lives. When we do not change our circumstances much, and neither do the people around us, lifelong friendship is a probability. Today, however, most of us have available choices and options undreamed of even fifty years ago. We can embark on two or three careers within a lifetime (not only can but may have to); sample from a cornucopia of leisure-time activities; resume school in middle age; divorce, cohabitate, engage in homosexual marriages, join communes, make radical changes in the direction of our lives—all with little or no onus. Though I shall discuss mobility in relation to fading friendships rather specifically in the next chapter, it's also a causative factor in our change of friends: simply because of population growth we encounter many more people who move even if we don't; and mobility in the workplace is much higher than what it was.

We are never at thirty-six what we were at sixteen, but in an earlier day the differences were not as sharp as they are now; furthermore, it was more likely in the past that we and our friends would continue to grow in the same direction and at more or less the same pace. We can no longer count on that happening. It is more rare than usual for life circumstances to be similar and to produce similar changes in two friends.

Even situations seemingly ready-made for lifelong commitment can easily fall apart because the earlier symmetry no longer exists. You would think that when soldiers fight and drink and whore around together for a few years, and become as close as brothers, they would continue to be buddies after their discharge from the service. I interviewed fifty-seven ex-servicemen through the United States and only six could say they still saw *any* of the buddies they had while in the service. "After we got out we all scattered," I was to hear repeatedly, but in many cases those former friends lived within easy driving range of my interviewees. More to the point, close service friends do things together they may not want to remember later on; are more revealing with each other than ever before or since ("You tell your buddy in the service things you didn't tell anyone else," is the way one ex-GI put it)—and don't want to be reminded of it. If they went through the hell of combat together they may not want to be reminded of that, either. Horrendous experiences of all kinds, which bring people into the closest of contact, can easily produce reactions negative to the relationships once the episode is over. Typical is the outcome of a cave-in in a Canadian coal mine a few years ago: entombed for eight days before their rescue, according to sociologist Rex Lucas, the trapped miners cried in front of each other and comforted each other. Six months later they were embarrassed if they encountered each other in any situation more formal than a casual, accidental meeting on the street.

Such circumstances are extreme and revolve around friendships formed in very specific and unusual situations, but they do sharply illustrate the principle of reciprocal satisfaction of needs bringing people together and the end of that reciprocity (no longer needing to have those needs filled) causing an end to the relationship.

That our friendships end when our "usefulness" to each other is over is nothing new; they debated about that in Aristotle's day. If it seems callous it is only because I have put it so baldly; experts in children's behavior frequently counsel parents against insisting that their children remain friends with other children even though they have outgrown them; adults, too, "outgrow" their friends, sometimes literally, sometimes merely in the sense of lives taking different turns. Friendships have always faded when the two friends have had less in common and saw each other less and less. What is new is that the fading of friendships is a much more rapid and repetitious process than it used to be.

I am not suggesting that we should view each other as disposable in the way paper napkins are disposable, only that what may seem like a depressing parade of people in and out of our lives might rather more helpfully be seen as an inevitable consequence of the opportunity for growth and change. In practical terms, we don't generally "throw each other away," as we are sometimes accused of doing; we simply go through a natural, ongoing process of selection and reselection.

To be sure, this has its costs. It has its painful moments. "I don't even put people's names in my address book, I just Scotch-tape them in," a free-lance editor in his thirties told me. It was hyperbole, but he was making a point, too. But then he also told me that he had gone through several profound changes in his life-style already—from straight college student to hippie freak to a productive life involving many interesting people. Everything must be seen in an individualistic context: change can mean growth, but it can also mean running and running in an avoidance of self. We must each decide for ourselves how rapidly we want to engage in change in our lives, and balance the costs. Even breaking off a friendship that has become destructive to us can easily be a painful experience: we have invested much of ourselves in the friend, so there is the loss not only of the other but of oneself in the other.

Wanting to avoid the painfully slow withering of a relationship they know is on the downgrade, some people—often but not only teenagers—precipitate bitter quarrels to get the whole thing over with at once. It provides the excuse for a break but it certainly dodges the issues surrounding the unknotting of that friendship tie, and that is a pity: we can learn as much about ourselves from the breakup of a friendship in its prime. Also in trying to avoid pain, many of us tend to downgrade a friendship that has ended, as if to say, "Well, it didn't really matter, anyway." But it did matter or we wouldn't be so vehement about it; to negate the goodness of a friendship that has ended is to be unfair to ourselves as well as to the friend in question—it means robbing ourselves of the joyful, enriching part of the friendship, and it means denying all the good feelings we have had about the relationship. We all find ways of preventing pain, of course, but the important thing is when and how: at times attempting avoidance of pain can be avoidance of life itself.

The more dimensions there are to a friendship the less likely it is to fall apart. However, the more dimensions there are the more painful a break, should one occur, is apt to be. Also the more guilt-producing. Guilt is far from an uncommon emotion in the wake of a broken or faded friendship, especially if the friends were very close at one time. There is the thought, "I'm betraying the friendship by no longer feeling good about it—I'm being disloyal." But betrayal or disloyalty really has nothing to do with the legitimacy of one's feelings—or lack of feelings, as the case may be. The dictionary meaning of loyalty is "feelings of devoted attachment and affection," something clearly no longer an issue if we are willing to end a friendship or have it fade away. Loyalty has to do with empathy and honesty and concern and discretion and not being hypocritical. What is called loyalty sometimes is more a rationalization for hanging on to a friendship one feels quite ambivalent about: feeling good about oneself for sticking with the friend, perhaps, or preferring to keep on with the relationship rather than take the risk of being alone or of striking out to find new friends. It's not unusual to hang on to an old friendship (especially as one grows older), even if it is a largely boring one—because it is also comfortable, because it is safe. But that has nothing to do with loyalty.

Longevity is no guarantee of goodness any more than a friendship of fairly short duration has, by its very nature, to be tentative. Changes are disruptive of friendships but changes also enhance our opportunities for friendship in the sense that we become exposed to more people. If, as communications expert Stanley Milgram estimates, each of us today has a pool of anywhere from 500 to 2500 acquaintances, it means a tremendous job of sorting out who is important and who is not, whom we can give time to and who must be avoided; otherwise we would drown in a sea of interaction with people. But it also means tremendously enlarged chances of finding friends who do "fit." Jerry, one of my respondents, put it neatly. He talked of his life as a very young man in a small town near Austin, Texas, and then of his decision to come to New York City, where he had lived for about a year when I met him. He said, "When I was younger my friends were my friends because—well, simply because we lived near each other. We were stuck with each other. Now making friends is like picking beautiful flowers in my garden of people. I have a choice."

15

New Networks for Old

THERE is much more to be said about our changing society and its impact on friendships—about the way American friendship patterns have been and about the way they are going. Throughout, my point will be that issues relating to friendship often are seen too simply; that we can understand them fully only when we view them from several perspectives. And then things turn out not always to be what they seem.

Neighborhood friends is a case in point. Many of us have really warm, nostalgic feelings about the traditional neighborhood: older folks sitting on stoops, kids playing on the street, mama-papa stores, a community feeling . . . and all of it gone.

Well, it is *not* all gone; there are still lots of city enclaves, for instance, where adults sit on stoops and kids hang out on the streets—only the faces now tend to be black or the voices Spanish-speaking, so to ethnic whites who made good and moved away to the suburbs it just seems as if they're gone. And some small towns have somehow managed to preserve their serenity despite creeping (or hurrying) urbanization all about, and neighbors are friends as always.

Still, America is a land transformed: hi-rise apartment houses simply are not evocative of the kind of chummy feeling that exists where there are smaller-scale buildings and friendship networks are well established. Many residents describe those hi-risers as cold, as filled with people who come and go—not as places where one readily makes friends. An interesting study by William Michaelson of the University of Toronto, whose Centre for Urban and Community Studies is doing a good deal of imaginative work in the field, suggests that people in hi-risers are more likely than people living in houses to see their neighbors in a negative light. Even if one has a friend or two in the building, it is only two out of, say, one hundred people living there—whereas on a typical street of one-story houses one might know seven or eight families of a possible fourteen or so. Not only are local contacts much fewer in the hi-rise; even the impact of those one knows is reduced because of the proportions involved.

America is a land transformed: a thirty-acre suburban shopping center dotted with supermarkets and stores of all kinds does not evoke feelings of friendliness and neighborliness, either—especially in contrast to the neighborhood stores of old. A number of middle-aged interviewees in suburban communities talked with a great deal of feeling about the way things were when they were kids; when going to the butcher for a piece of meat was not a cut-and-dried transaction but an experience filled with humanity: "We visited, my Mom and I, when we went to the butcher, we talked about our respective families, we gossiped—it wasn't just a matter of buying lamb chops, we *cared* about each other," said a well-off industrial engineer in Los Angeles' sprawling San Fernando Valley. Often more was involved than the difference between a neighborly chat on the one hand and a hurried exchange with a busy supermarket cashier on the other. For some people, not only but especially for those who had trouble getting close to other people, store visits (and chats with neighbors) constituted an integral part of the whole friendship process. They were nourished by the exchanges. Those exchanges might have been enough for them. To the extent that the opportunity for such conversations is diminished, they feel diminished.

However, before we despair entirely about the passing of the traditional neighborhood, we can look at the phenomenon from other perspectives. First, a closer look at suburban neighborhoods and friendships, then city ones. Initially, in the early 1950s, the suburbs really came in for a heavy shelling from some outraged social critics. Their main thrust: suburbanites are all alike; they all want to do the same things; they mingle only with each other. In short, suburbanites were accused of being too friendly with each other (though it was never put so positively).

Now one hardly hears such criticisms any more. One reason is that some perceptive sociologists and other social observers—Herbert J. Gans is one—have shown that suburbs are not so homogeneous as an outward glance at boxy, look-alike houses might suggest. Second, imbued with the pioneer spirit, families moving into new developments turned fervently to each other. In time there occurred an inevitable shaking out; people became more selective about their neighborhood friends—and, too, the original spirit of togetherness further weakened as some residents moved out and newcomers arrived and eventually moved out themselves. Thus a friendly neighborhood becomes less friendly.

But whether or not such a metamorphosis takes place, there are more and less friendly neighborhoods, more or fewer opportunities to make local friends. To some extent this is a case of friendliness, like beauty, being in the eye of the beholder. I talked with two men, one right after the other, about the same Minneapolis suburb in which both lived. One man lauded its friendliness; the other condemned it as being cold and unfriendly. Were they really talking about the identical locale? Yes—it developed that the second man was in vehement disagreement with the prevailing attitudes in that particular community; there was distinct dissonance between man and place.

People often check out neighborhood schools when they move into a community, but they do not check out the "friendship quotient." I think this is a mistake. Suburbs, portions of suburbs, even streets, vary one from the other in terms of general friendliness and acceptance of newcomers. Some residents are eager to make friends. But others—quite a few—do not want to get too chummy with their neighbors. This is very much the case with some middle- and upper-middle-class people (working-class persons often make little distinction between "friend" and "neighbor"). Money in itself is a distancing factor; the more one has the less one wants other people to know too much about oneself. Moving from lower- to middle-class surroundings can produce a rejection of the old neighborhood feeling in another way, too: here I had all these neighbors on top of me before, I had no choice about my crowded living conditions; now I have the choice, I can create a little separateness between me and the people next door.

Individuals in executive positions and in academic and other jobs where intrigue at work is not an unknown element very quickly become sensitive to people "knowing too much" about them and extend that to their home grounds, too: for instance, a study of seventy-five Middle Western executives, undertaken in the 1950s, makes this very clear. Asked to give their definition of the "good neighbor," they replied: somebody who helps out in an emergency; somebody with whom you can establish a mutual aid pattern ("Watch my kids, please, while I run down to the market for a minute"); somebody with whom you have exchange borrowing privileges; somebody to have an occasional drink or barbecue with; somebody who's friendly but not too friendly and above all respects your privacy. Only four of the men interviewed numbered some close friends among their neighbors.

Quite a few people would go along with the definition the majority of those executives gave, I think, and not just out of wariness: if you're close friends with a neighbor and the friendship breaks up, how can you go on living in close proximity to each other? Better not get too involved in the first place. In Southern California I noticed six-foot backyard fences as more the rule than the exception, and the reason for them is not unfriendliness but the wish for privacy: backyards are extensions of the living room or the playroom in that balmy climate, and as one suntanned homeowner put it, who wants to have neighbors peering into your living room?

Also, suburban neighborhoods, though never as homogeneous as was assumed, are becoming more heterogeneous than ever. On the same block of $35,000 homes it is far from unusual to find living there a scientist, a fireman, a schoolteacher, the owner of a hardware store, an office manager, and a couple in retirement, say —each of them with different interests and life-styles. "We don't have that much in common with our neighbors any more" was far from an infrequent comment by suburbanities when we discussed neighbors and friends. It is the old story of like seeking like, of preferring to meet and be friends with strangers who are not so very strange after all.

For these and other reasons many suburban homeowners do not form the bulk of their friendships locally. Their cars enable them to transcend distance; most of their friends live a mile, five miles, ten miles—and, in places like Texas and California, where distances are irrelevant except in case of gasoline shortages—even thirty or more miles away, visiting back and forth regularly. Propinquity, the primary element in the way friendships used to be formed, is becoming irrelevant.

This does not prevent some of us from bemoaning the passing of the old neighborhood friendships. We knew their warmth, their comfortableness, and genuinely miss them. Nostalgia aside, however, how much do we really miss them? Apparently not enough to reproduce them impressively in our current circumstances. Nor do we seem overly enthusiastic about getting more of a taste of the kinds of lives we used to have: most people, revisiting the old city neighborhoods or the small towns of their origins once a year, return home with the feeling, "It was great to go back—but once a year is enough!" Then why the nostalgia? Maybe, unreasonably, we want it all: the old-fashioned rootedness, but without its limitations; the modern privacy, but without the cost; the farmhouse, just as long as there's a shopping center five minutes away.

At the heart of the decline of neighborhood friendships is the fact that we have those greatly enlarged opportunities to make friends elsewhere. Because of our cars we can take advantage of those opportunities; as the last chapter indicated, the opportunities themselves have come about because of changes in people's lifestyles. The time-honored custom of the "kaffeeklatsch"—suburban housewives dropping in on their neighbors for coffee and gossip after hubbies and children are safely off on the day's activities—provides a striking example. Almost everywhere I explored friendship patterns in middle-class suburban circles the kaffeeklatsch is sharply on the wane. Have the women who stopped participating suddenly turned away from their neighbors? Not exactly; more to the point, they have expanded their horizons. They are no longer isolated in the neighborhood all day long; expanded child-care facilities, but more importantly their own drive, have brought them back to school, to work, to arts-and-crafts centers, to community work and other activities—in effect, to a more directional use of their time in places outside the neighborhood, where they meet new, stimulating friends.

When we look at city people, the deep-seated changes that have been occurring in American friendship patterns come into really sharp focus. Both in the social-science and in popular literature, urbanites have always been depicted in the most depressing of terms: faceless people lost in the crowds of surging humanity; blindly, anonymously stumbling about their disconnected way; not bound by a common tradition, consequently only weakly tied to other people (if tied at all), epitomes of alienation and isolation in mass society. Urbanites are also depicted as having to ward off contact with others, and to keep their relationships as superficial as possible, because there are so many people around that otherwise one would drown in them. The truth is rather less dramatic, though not without its own excitement. Of course there are plenty of lonely people cooped up in rat warrens as well as luxury hirisers, just as there are lonely people everywhere. And because of the abundance of people, encounters with the many are kept relatively swift and superficial—which enables the urbanite, as Harvey Cox points out in *The Secular City*, to retain enough psychic energy to cultivate deeper friendships with the few. Poor people in cities are supposed to be especially bereft of friendships; numerous studies contradict this thesis. One such, of the black ghetto of the Roxbury district of Boston, for instance, shows that eight out of ten residents see their friends three times a week or more; a study of black street-corner men in Washington, D.C., shows how carefully they structure their world specifically to include friends who provide companionship and support. City youth gangs are far more than centers for delinquent activity; they have evolved as well-developed social systems specifically geared to cope with isolation. Poor or well off, what urbanites lack in the way of small-town warmth—and numerous city enclaves do not lack it—they balance off by the greater amount of privacy and variety of potential friends they have available.

Men and women who live in large apartment buildings often say they hardly know who their next-door neighbors are, much less those living a few doors down the hall; people come and go and barely a "hello" is said in between. Like suburbanites in neighborhoods that lack outgoingness, these apartment dwellers might find one or two congenial people (or families) in the building to be neighborly with, or to have as friends—but propinquity is almost an afterthought. They first meet because they do live in the same building, of course, and it does give one a more comfortable feeling to have someone in the building to be friendly with. But the strong drawing power is the things they have in common—and if there is no one in the building or on the block they have something in common with, it does not neccessarily follow that they are lonely. They have friends, but their friends are scattered around.

There's the crux of the shift in American friendship patterns: friends are all over, but they are really not "scattered" haphazardly, even though it might seem that way. Whereas traditional friendship networks were spatially based—that is, encompassed by specific geographical boundaries like neighborhoods or workplaces—we are transcending space. We are building communities for ourselves based primarily on personal considerations such as congeniality and compatibility of interests in areas like sports, hobbies, recreational pursuits, and the like—and as a result accomplishing what urban planners call "despatialization of communities." If the typical city dweller is measured by the number of local friends he has, in many instances he might seem to be isolated. But if he is measured by his "personal communities," as Barry Wellman of the Centre for Urban and Community Studies calls them, he is far from isolated. (For a growing number of the employed—especially executives, educators, and scientific researchers—the idea of "work friends" as being related to one's central place of business also has to be modified. Many of these people travel to so many meetings, seminars, conferences, and symposiums, where they keep running into the same people, that their work friends or colleagues are truly scattered all over—yet form a very definable network from the point of view of dovetailing professional interests.)

The supposed isolation of city dwellers also underestimates their capacity to weld into fairly solid "communities" in the face of threatening situations, real or imagined, such as deteriorating schools or the proposed erection of drug treatment centers. "Unfriendly" as well as "friendly" suburbs too show this capacity to form communities—albeit sometimes warring communities—in the face of external threats to the neighborhood. Though such communities disband after the emergency has passed, some friendships continue: the people involved have really discovered each other.

Even if our friends are not restricted to a particular neighborhood or section of town, our relationships with them will be affected, of course, if they or we move out of the city. Chapter 2 made clear that mobility is nothing new in American life and that the extent of it has been exaggerated. Roughly 80 per cent of Americans who move remain in the same geographical area; roughly two thirds do not even leave their city or town. The experiences of executives or military men and their families are usually cited to show the destructive elements of mobile life-styles. Many such people are transferred every two or three years, but most of us are not executives or in the military. Census Bureau figures show that overall we are actually a bit less mobile in recent years than we were before. Nevertheless, 31.7 per cent of all Americans changed their residences during a three-year period ending in March 1973, and that represents a lot of friendships affected one way or the other by people's moving.

Shifting one's residence from one city to another can be a joy (if one wants to get away or if the move is a step upward socioeconomically); it also always involves a certain amount of stress. When we move we must disband our households, leave familiar surroundings, say goodbye to family and friends, establish ourselves in the new locale, learn its customs and expectations, work ourselves into new social networks.

The stress is greater for some categories of people than it is for others. Teenagers, caught up in best-friendships or tight little cliques, are usually hit hard by the prospect of moving elsewhere; it is much more difficult for them than for younger children. Corporation wives often feel a sense of isolation in their new communities that their husbands do not feel—their husbands, after all, immediately become caught up in the office society. The more radical the change in life-styles resulting from a move, the more traumatic the initial adjustment period is likely to be—moving from a rural area to the big city, for example, frequently subjects the mover to a massive culture shock.

Families that are internally stable and accustomed to enjoyable social participation find it far easier to make friends in their new communities than do families in conflict and/or families that habitually have been more isolated. It should be noted that most studies reflecting a poor adjustment in terms of the interpersonal relationships of those who move have come from mental-health clinicians—those who work with troubled individuals and families. This is clearly a skewed sample from which to extrapolate to the population in general. Very recent sociological studies, focusing on nonclinical samplings of movers, offer some commonsense conclusions: moving is stressful for everybody, but the degree of stress depends on a host of factors—including the emotional meaning that the move has for the persons involved, the stability of the movers as individuals and family members, how adequately the move has been prepared for, how outgoing the family is, how readily members will join local clubs, churches, civic organizations, PTAs, and the like.

What happens to existing friendships once one of the friends moves away? The question hardly lends itself to any broad generalizations. Without question there is a good deal of "out of sight, out of mind"—especially in the case of people who cannot or do not wish to make strong commitments in their friendships. Often an initial exchange of letters or phone calls dwindles to nothing as the people who have moved get caught up in their new environments. Even a move from city to suburb, implying that distances are not too great, nevertheless results in an eventual cutting off of former relationships. Returning to the city becomes an "expedition," as many suburbanites put it; there may also be a subtle disengagement process at work: a shift of allegiance to the new locale, as it were. When Herbert J. Gans, the sociologist, investigated the social life of families that had moved into a New Jersey Levittown housing development some years ago, he found that overwhelmingly they shifted the focus of their social life to the new community even though Philadelphia, where many of them had come from, was only twenty miles away. When I interviewed residents of an "adult community" in Silver Springs, Maryland, I also found that most of them were seldom seeing friends they had left behind.

Nevertheless, I encountered a perhaps surprising number of people who do keep in touch, who visit each other regularly, and who make ample use of mails and telephone in the service of the friendship. Not infrequently one of the two friends, rather than both, made special efforts to maintain the relationship—but even the more passive involvement of the other indicated a need to prevent the friendship from lapsing.

An important qualification is in order here. That a friendship is allowed to lapse does not necessarily mean the *spirit* of the friendship is no more. We involve ourselves in our friendships on the plane of substance and reality; we also live them on the plane of feeling, fantasy, and fond (or not so fond) remembrance. There is the friend in the here and now; there is the internalized friend who is part of our past, part of our history. It is true, for instance, that the Levittowners did not see their old friends; it is not true that those friends they had left behind upon moving were "dead" for them. Gans, who lived in the community for the initial two years of its existence as a participant-observer, noted, "Many Levittowners talk about close friends 'at home,' but they see them so rarely that the current strength of the friendship is never properly tested."

Gans is hardly alone in such observations. When social investigators N. Babchuk and A. P. Bates in Nebraska set about to learn some things about the friendship patterns of middle-class married couples there, they found that "couples talked about non-local friends in such vivid language that we thought such persons had only recently moved to other areas and were surprised, later in the interview, to find that there had been no face-to-face contact and little correspondence between some friends for years and years."

Is this a fiction some of us need to create, this closeness with friends from the past? I think not. The authors of the Nebraska study call these faraway but inwardly present friends "members of suspended primary groups," adding that, given our mobility, we must produce a lot of such groups. But if "suspended" is synonymous with "inactive," the impression I gained was that such friends are not inactive, not suspended. Like close friends who die but remain with us still, close friends from whom we are separated because of a move remain rich and meaningful presences at times. They constitute yet another network of real friends, unseen but not unfelt.

Among my respondents, only one third of the men but 60 per cent of the women said their friendships do not diminish in intensity when a geographical separation occurs. This probably reflects the tendency of women to establish stronger emotional ties. Some respondents, both women and men, said that when they met their friends again after a long interval there was nothing left of the old spark between them; they had changed in too many divergent ways. Almost everyone, however, had gone through the joyous experience of meeting old friends again after a long separation and finding that no matter how many actual months or years had gone by, the separation was really of no more than a heartbeat's duration; very quickly, after just a bit of testing, they could pick up again where they had left off. Such experiences affirm us in our ability to judge people; more importantly, they confirm our places in a network that transcends geography and time, and is bounded only by the parameters of receptivity and affection.

Social scientists have repeatedly observed, of people who move a great deal throughout their lifetimes, that they stop being receptive to close friendships. That they acquire a malady called "rootlessness." They no longer want to plant roots, as it were, because those roots will only be torn up again in a year or two or three. They form friendships but avoid becoming too committed. In effect, a subtle psychological change occurs over time—in the direction of their putting greater distance between themselves and other people. It is how they protect themselves from the pain of having to keep on saying goodbye.

There is no question but that this occurs much of the time among habitual movers. There is, however, good cause to question whether, as the critics contend, this is an inevitable consequence of high mobility. It does not happen to everyone. As you will see, there are people who adopt an alternative response to the seminomadic life. Is the withdrawal that takes place, then, only connected with transiency, or are there other factors involved? Do people who react this way have a single, undeviating ideal of friendship in mind—the traditional, everlasting kind—and are they unable to shake loose from that ideal? Is it that they generally keep people at a bit of a distance but then, upon being asked whether moving affects their relationships, seize upon this factor to explain the distance between themselves and others? Families subject to many moves are sometimes families in tension because the husbands and fathers involved have an overriding commitment to their work, giving little emotionally to their wives and children—could that be a factor?

Military families are suggestive: an Air Force psychiatrist told me that the well-traveled Air Force officer who treats his family like "little tribes members" usually has withdrawn, taciturn children—but that stable families, in which there is togetherness, are better able to adjust to the mobile life and the children are not withdrawn. A study of U.S. Army families in Germany very clearly shows that the wife with personal and family problems, who identifies poorly with the service life, has a very limited social life before as well as after her move; conversely, the well-adjusted Army wife is able to reintegrate herself "into the informal community of friendship and support" after a move.

Far from cooling off their friendships in reaction to the knowledge that they will have to say goodbye, a small but growing number of people, I believe, are heating them up. That is, they are speeding up the process of turning strangers into friends, breaking the barriers sooner, as if to say, "I know that in time I'll have to leave, so let's get the most enjoyment out of each other that we can while we're together." In *Future Shock,* Alvin Toffler discusses the friendships of the future, suggesting that changing interests, shifting allegiance to subgroups, and mobility will create "friendship patterns . . . for many satisfactions," and substitute "many close relationships of shorter durability for the few long-term friendships formed in the past." Actually, such friendship patterns are not off somewhere in the distance but upon us today. In response to all kinds of changes—of residence, of interests, of employment, of life-styles—and under the influence of certain liberating influences, some people are in effect already being shaped to adopt such patterns.

Speeded-up friendships are nothing new. We speed them up while on vacations, knowing that very quickly we must part from these new friends. College and service friendships are formed subject to time limitations. Under such circumstances we do not generally *think* about having a limited amount of time together; we simply react to that reality. Of course, vacation, college, and service environments have their own special ambiance, aside from time considerations, that help to break down barriers sooner—but the point is that we do break them, and a minority of us are already doing so in more general circumstances.

Darien, Connecticut, a residential haven for transient executives, is a case in point. Upon first arriving, many of their wives join the YWCA-run Newcomers Club, which enables them to make friends quickly (most often with other members), helps integrate them into the community, and offers social functions for themselves and their husbands. Investigating the friendship patterns of these very mobile wives, some of them already having moved twelve or fourteen times, I learned that many are resistant to forming close friendships; they know they will move again. But a minority among them—almost wholly younger women who are in consciousness-raising groups—do not let the idea of having to say goodbye inhibit them; they have quickly formed intense friendships.

Southern California, always identified with soaring mobility rates, is another case in point. Talking to family-service workers all over the area, I had no trouble collecting case histories of highly mobile people whose friendships are superficial and whose family relationships are shaky. But I also heard about numerous other families that take their moves in stride or even thrive on them. They plunge right into church, school, and volunteer activities, make friends quickly and spontaneously, and on some cases—for instance, those joining Pentecostal-evangelical church groups— become members of social circles characterized by a family kind of warmth and sharing.

16

The American Way
of Friendship

A NUMBER of my interviewees, foreign and American, referred
to the past—the "good old days"—when everything was better,
when friendships were deeper, stronger, longer-lasting, more
committed. Of course, ever since human beings could reckon the
difference between past and present, the past has seemed safer,
easier, more secure. Nostalgia always lends enchantment; why
should it be different with respect to friendships?

Small-town America is fondly remembered as a place where
your adult friends had been your childhood friends, where everybody knew everybody else, where stability and commitment and a
kind of group protectiveness—the aura of one big happy family—
reigned supreme. So it was for some people, though of course
family members too have their hostilities and bitter rifts. More to
the point, what was safety and warmth for some was stifling
conformity for others, who fled or disassociated themselves from
the community. Class divisions were much sharper than in the
cities. If you failed to conform to the mores that prevailed—or you
or your family hadn't lived there for three dozen years—you were

an outsider. (Something still true today, I kept hearing from numerous city people who have moved into smallish towns at the edges of exurbia to live or work.) Everybody was helpful if you needed help, though you weren't expected to parade your troubles around. Lots of things people didn't talk about, except via the ever-present underground gossip machine; many people learned more about their friends behind their backs than face to face.

The past? Take a quick look at "Middletown"—actually Muncie, Indiana—the subject of a classic sociological study when it was a town of under 50,000 in the mid-1920s. The sociologist team conducting the study found that a third of the working-class wives and one in eight of the businessmen's wives interviewed said they either had no friends at all in town or no "intimate" friends. "We've let all our friends slip away as our children have taken up more and more of our time," explained one of the more isolated businessmen's wives, echoing a refrain heard from some of the others. But even those of the women who talked about having friends also talked about what they saw as a decline in friendships: "I don't see my friends at all. That is really true—I never see them unless I run into them somewhere occasionally or they come over to dinner. It was different with my mother. She and her friends were always in each other's houses," said one such lady.

I couldn't help wondering: would that woman's mother also have talked about deteriorating friendships had she been interviewed in her day? At any rate, over a decade later, in the middle of the Depression, the sociologists were back in Middletown for a follow-up study. Maybe they expected people in the midst of hard times to be more friendly and intimate with each other. What they found was that people were more suspicious of each other. Fences were higher. Class distinctions were more pronounced. There were fallings out between people who had lost everything and people who had not.

Also in the past, though admittedly the more recent past, is a study of friendship in Eugene, Oregon. In the early 1950s behavioral scientists and students from the University of Oregon interviewed 400 persons in and around Eugene, which then had a population of around 100,000. And what did the interviewers find? They found a bare handful of people—six, to be exact—who would admit to feeling badly if they lost touch with their best friends. And all of those were women!

In 1972 a guest columnist in *The New York Times* began a short column on community with, "Intimacy is a declining national resource." But I simply fail to get a sense of intimacy, of friendship, being so highly prized in the past, in our American past. The subject was not of concern to the Puritans; one scholar, Professor William A. Sadler, suggests the reason was God: if people put confidence in friends they would put less confidence in God "and thereby offend him." Certainly, our Calvinist, work-ethic approach to life—keep a stiff upper lip, be self-sufficient, hold feelings in check—has not been conducive to the flowering of intimate contact.

In fact, only now are we beginning to reach out. Only now are we beginning to think about such things as intimacy *as a value to aspire to.* (Probably no coincidence: most of us having gone beyond achieving the material necessities of life, we can "afford" to begin to think of other things.) The whole "human liberation" movement, from civil rights to the sexual revolution to women's and gay rights groups, is having its impact on all of us, I believe, to think more deeply about ourselves and our needs. For the first time we—not only philosophers, clergymen, or social scientists, but the collective ordinary-man-and-woman "we"—are starting to ask some really penetrating questions about the nature of our ties and the meaning they hold for us. To ask them not only silently, within the confines of our inner selves, or very privately, in the company of a trusted person or two, but out in the open, publicly, where all of us must hear and none of us can wholly escape looking at the implications as they concern us.

How, then, to explain the fact that some of the people who were to discuss friendship with me discussed loneliness instead? How to fit in the men and women—quite a few college students among them—who said how difficult it was to find friends to open up to?

Loneliness is a terribly complicated issue, for it encompasses the plight of the very shy person; the highly competitive person; the person who has lost a loved one; the person thrust in alien surroundings; the person who is forever seeking to fulfill impossible ideals of love and friendship; as well as the existential loneliness we all feel from time to time, and more or less keenly—the loneliness springing from the realization that the experiences of birth, life, and death, the very experiences that bind us to other human beings, are also the ones we must ultimately experience in separateness.

If we find it difficult to encounter the kinds of friends we can "open up to," it may be that basically we do not want to meet such people, do not want to risk any emotional unfolding. Or it may be more complicated than that: that heretofore we have been in the situation of people who do not miss what they don't have and don't know about. If intimacy is a value we are just starting to know about—to think seriously about in relation to ourselves—we certainly now do realize we are missing something. And that realization can be quite a painful, scary one.

Yet that very realization, despite all its pain, embodies in it a profoundly hopeful and optimistic note: that we *do* want more openness and warmth in our relationships, and—just as important —that we feel comfortable enough about this want to acknowledge and articulate it. It is possible to run away from the implications involved and many persons certainly do run from the prospect of intimacy as if it were an emotional plague—but it is also possible to proceed from realization to learning: the slow and sometimes exhausting process of learning to trust ourselves and the validity of our needs more, to trust other people more, and of learning the psychic and social skills necessary to get what we say we want.

The popularity of encounter, sensitivity, and "growth" groups is dramatic evidence of our desire to learn those skills. It is a fallacy to think that we can achieve the capacity to be intimate in a weekend marathon or even after a couple of months' worth of effort. Moreover, many such groups are seriously deficient both in the adequacy of their leadership and in their overall methodological approach. But while the promise of "instant intimacy" is a cruel hoax, the more effective techniques have been adopted by other, more orthodox, mental-health disciplines and, at its best, the movement suggests and tries to arouse the potential we have for relating more deeply to ourselves and others.

Communes produce more evidence of our reaching out. The modern communal movement has enjoyed a tremendous increase in popularity since the mid-1960s; while even the most thorough of researchers can only guess at the number of communes around, it is estimated that as many as three out of every 1000 Americans are now living in urban or rural communes and communal arrangements. Though there are some middle-aged and older communards, most are in their late teens and in their twenties. For many communards the commune experience is a passing phase; Mathew Greenwald, a young sociologist who has studied urban communes, estimates that the average length of stay is one year and that some communes—especially those started by college students—last only a few months, from September to June.

Contrary to popular belief, communes vary considerably each from the other in terms of both their ethos and their approach. A host of reasons, many having nothing to do with friendship or relatedness in general, bring people to particular communes: it is a practical way of living very cheaply; there may be opportunities for sexual sharing; some communes provide the chance for personal growth or religious experience; some are established for specific political or professional purposes (there are communes dedicated to the overthrow of the government, and communes run by activist lawyers on behalf of the poor.)

Yet the idea of being in closer contact with others is an underlying motivation for many communards whose main goals are of a more practical nature, and a specific inducement for others. Singles whose life experiences have led them to equate commitment with possessiveness, especially in their sexual-romantic attachments, are drawn to communes because they can enjoy sexual and emotional intimacy to the degree they feel comfortable with it, without having to be paired with one person. And some communes very specifically call themselves "family," or have the word "family" in their names; they endeavor to provide alternatives to what they see as outmoded and restricting traditional family life. In effect, they are trying to learn to live together in an innovative form of the extended family.

Whether we are young or older, in or out of communes, our friends are becoming more like extended family, in certain ways replacing or substituting for the aunts, uncles, cousins, grandparents, and other family members who comprised the larger extended family of old. We have always likened especially close friends to family—"He's like a brother to me," or, "She's more like a sister to me than my own sister is"—to indicate the degree of closeness that exists. What is new is that in a structural sense, too, we are making increased use of each other as family. It is a phenomenon that is cutting across age groups and socioeconomic levels. Black youths in the ghettos of New York, Washington, D.C., and elsewhere pack a few things and show up at friends' homes, where they hole up for a few weeks when things get to be too rough at home. At times middle-class teenagers in the suburbs use friends' homes as crash pads to escape family pressures. The street-corner men of Washington, D.C., consciously make kinspeople out of friends—"going for brothers" or, in the case of cross-sex but platonic friendships, "going for cousins." Middle-class families are making more conscious use of close family friends—whose values are similar to their own—to help instill those values in their children, which is a function formerly performed for the most part by real family members. In effect, they build "social subsystems," as a study of "successful families" puts it, to aid them in emphasizing and reinforcing the principles and standards they want their children to adopt. More parents who are arranging for legal guardianship for their children should they die are, I am told, choosing friends over relatives than was the case before.

The family of blood and marriage ties is an economic as well as a social unit, and we are making more economic use of our family-friends and they of us. More and more we are pooling resources with our friends to buy goods and services we could not afford unilaterally—luxury items like boats and summer houses, for instance; taking trips together as families and sharing expenses; even living together the year round. Not quite communally, but certainly not conventionally, a growing number of families who feel close to each other are buying or renting large houses together for all-year living. With separate bedrooms and bathrooms they have the privacy they usually want; other facilities are pooled. In some instances professionals are meshing their work lives as well as their personal lives—for instance, activist lawyers, doctors, and psychologists. In California I interviewed a practicing psychologist who is pooling resources with seven colleagues and their families. They have bought a large tract of beautiful wooded land, they are building individual homes as well as communal recreation and eating facilities, they will engage in a joint practice and share lives—"I'm eleven years older than my wife, and neither of our real families provide the kind of emotional values we believe in," the psychologist said by way of added explanation. "I want to know she'll always have a family she can trust and feel comfortable with."

In such ways is the line between traditional friendship and kinship blurring and, I think, will continue to blur as we form our little islands of community in a sea of social change. I think we are moving in the direction of more openness, more cognizance of the value of friendship. I know our approach to friendship, as a society, is the most difficult of all. We lack specific societal guidelines—guidelines that could tell us what we must and must not do in our relationships with friends—that could help us conform to a common ideal of friendship. Most of us lack cultural supports in relation to our friendships—supports that could help shape our expectations and our standards; they are weakening even among ethnic groups where they once were strong.

We are on our own, we and our friends. We make our way, in this most remarkable of relationships, as we go along. Not having the more patterned kinds of friendship still found to greater or lesser degree elsewhere, we also do not have the kind of security that comes with knowing more or less specifically how things are and will be between ourselves and our friends. While poor friends, hypocritical friends, fair-weather friends, are found everywhere, we run a greater risk of disappointment and of superficiality in our friendships. We, more than others, must deal with competitive elements as these negatively affect friendships.

In turn, we need concern ourselves less with the forms of friendship and direct more attention to the personalities involved. Our friendships can be more spontaneous, more individualistic, more consistent with our mutual needs.

Books on friendship generally concern themselves with instruction—"how to" make friends—or are highly inspirational in tone, drawing their stimulation from the wisdom of the past. I came away from my research convinced that what would be most helpful to us now is not specific instruction or adherence to undeviating standards for friendship formed at a time quite unlike ours—what would be most helpful, I felt, would be for us to gain a greater awareness of the manifold ways in which our friendships affect and contribute to our lives. In the final analysis we must each be the architects of our own friendships, one after the other, and we must provide our own inspiration; this is the burden and the promise of American friendships as we are more and more pursuing them.

BIBLIOGRAPHY

Chapter 1

Burridge, Kenelm O. L. "Friendship in Tangu." *Oceania*, vol. 27, 1957, pp. 177–89.

Driberg, J. H. "The 'Best Friend' Among the Didinga." *Man*, July 1935, pp. 101–02.

Cicero, Marcus Tullius. *Cicero's Offices*. London: J. M. Dent & Sons, Ltd, 1966.

Great Books of the Western World. Vol. 25 *Montaigne*. New York: Encyclopaedia Britannica, 1952.

Chapter 2

Burridge, Kenelm O. L. *Op. cit.*

Carnegie, Dale. *How to Win Friends and Influence People*. New York: Pocket Books, 1972.

Gans, Herbert J. "Stimulus/Response: Vance Packard Misperceives the Way Most American Movers Live." *Psychology Today*, September 1972, pp. 20–28.

Gross, E. "Social Integration and the Control of Competition." *American Journal of Sociology*, 1961, 67, pp. 270–77.

La Rochefoucauld. *The Maxims of La Rochefoucauld*. New York: Modern Library, 1959.

Packard, Vance. *A Nation of Strangers*. New York: David McKay Company, Inc., 1972.

Paine, Robert. "In Search of Friendship: An Exploratory Analysis in 'Middle-class' Culture." *Man*, 1969, 4, pp. 505–24.

Piker, Steven. "Friendship to the Death in Rural Thai Society." *Human Organization*, vol. 27, no. 3 (Fall 1968).

Thernstrom, Stephan, and Sennett, Richard, eds. *Nineteenth Century Cities*. New Haven: Yale University Press, 1969.

Warner, W. Lloyd, and Lunt, Paul S. *The Social Life of a Modern Community*. New Haven: Yale University Press, 1941.

Chapter 3

Abrahams, R. D. "A Performance-centred Approach to Gossip." *Man*, vol. 5, no. 2 (June 1970), pp. 290–301.

Anonymous. "Alone in the Open Country." *Human Behavior*, May/June 1972, p. 63.

Eibl-Eibesfeldt, Irenaus. *Love and Hate.* New York: Holt, Rinehart and Winston, 1971.

Eisenstadt, S. N. "Ritualized Personal Relations." *Man*, no. 96 (July 1956), pp. 90–94.

Kreisman, D. E. "Social Interaction and Intimacy in Pre-schizophrenia." Ph.D. dissertation. Columbia University, 1969.

Langner, Thomas S., and Michael, Stanley T. *Life Stress and Mental Health.* London: The Free Press of Glencoe, 1963.

Lorenz, Konrad. *On Aggression.* New York: Harcourt, Brace & World, 1966.

Trumbull, H. C. *Friendship the Master Passion.* Philadelphia: John D. Wattles, 1892.

Useem, Michael. "Ideological and Interpersonal Change in the Radical Protest Movement." *Social Problems*, vol. 19, no. 4 (spring 1972).

Chapter 4

Bartolome, Fernando. "Executives As Human Beings." *Harvard Business Review*, November/December 1972, pp. 62–69.

Bradney, Pamela. "The Joking Relationship in Industry." *Human Relations*, vol. 10, 1957, pp. 179–87.

Emerson, R. W. *The Writings of Ralph Waldo Emerson.* New York: The Modern Library, 1940.

Maslow, A. H. *Motivation and Personality.* New York: Harper and Brothers, 1954.

Rangell, Leo. "On Friendship." *Journal of the American Psychoanalytic Association*, vol. 11, 1963, pp. 3–54.

Radcliffe-Brown, A. R. *Structure and Function in Primitive Society.* London: Cohen and West, 1952.

bibliography>>

Thomas, A., Chess, S., and Birch, H. G. "Origins of Personality." *Scientific American,* August 1970, pp. 102–09.

Thoreau, H. D. *Walden and Other Writings of Henry David Thoreau.* New York: The Modern Library, 1950.

Wyden, Barbara W. "The Difficult Baby Is Born That Way." *The New York Times Magazine,* March 21, 1971.

Chapter 5

Harlow, H. F. and M. "Learning to Love." *American Scientist,* 54, 3, 1966.

Hartup, Willard W. "Peer Interaction and Social Organization." In P. H. Mussen, ed., *Carmichael's Manual of Child Psychology.* New York: John Wiley & Sons, 1970.

Schaeffer, C. E. "A Psychological Study of Ten Exceptionally Creative Adolescent Girls." *Exceptional Children,* February 1970.

Watson, G. *Social Psychology.* New York: J. B. Lippincott Co., 1966.

Chapter 7

Anonymous. "Matched Pairs of Freshmen Score Higher." *Washington Post,* October 1, 1973.

Chapter 8

Ackerman, Charles. "Affiliations: Structural Determinants of Differential Divorce Rates." *American Journal of Sociology,* vol. 69 (July 1963), pp. 13–20.

Babchuck, Nicholas, and Bates, Alan P. "The Primary Relations of Middle-class Couples: A Study in Male Dominance." *American Sociological Review,* vol. 3, 1963, pp. 377–84.

Dotson, F. "Patterns of Voluntary Association Among Urban Working-class Families." *American Sociological Review,* vol. 16, no. 5 (October 1951), pp. 688–93.

Chapter 9

Blau, Zena S. "Changes in Status and Age Identification." *American Sociological Review,* vol. 21, no. 2, pp. 198–203.

Blau, Zena S. "Constraints on Friendships in Old Age." *American Sociological Review,* vol. 26, no. 3, pp. 429–439.

Gans, Herbert J. *The Levittowners.* New York: Pantheon Books, 1967.

Lowenthal, M. F., and Haven, C. "Interaction and Adaptation: Intimacy As a Critical Variable." *American Sociological Review*, vol. 33, no. 1, pp. 20–30.

Rosenberg, George S. *The Worker Grows Old.* San Francisco: Jossey-Bass, Inc., 1970.

Chapter 10

Beier, E. G., *et al.* "Similarity Plus Dissimilarity of Personality: Basis for Friendship?" *Psychological Reports,* 1961, 8, pp. 3–8.

Byrne, Donn. "Attitudes And Attraction." In L. Berkowitz, ed., *Advances in Experimental Social Psychology,* vol. 4.

Gerstl, Joel E. "Determinants of Occupational Community in High Status Occupations." *The Sociological Quarterly,* vol. 2, pp. 37–48.

Lazarsfeld, P. F., and Merton, R. K. "Friendship As Social Process: A Substantive and Methodological Analysis." In M. Berger *et al.*, eds., *Freedom and Control in Modern Society.* New York: Octagon Books, 1964.

Gans, Herbert J. *The Levittowners. Loc. cit.*

Watson, G. *Op. cit.*

Chapter 12

Booth, Alan. "Sex and Social Participation." *American Sociological Review,* vol. 37, 1972, pp. 183–92.

Gorer, Geoffrey. *The American People.* New York: W. W. Norton, Inc., 1964.

Gouldner, Helen B. *The Organization Woman: Patterns of Friendship and Organizational Commitment.* Ph.D. dissertation, Sociology Dept., UCLA, 1959.

Komarovsky, Mirra. *Blue-Collar Marriage.* New York: Random House, 1962.

Maurois, Andre. *The Art of Living.* New York: Harper & Row, 1959.

Morris, Desmond. *Intimate Behavior.* New York: Random House, 1972.

Tiger, Lionel. *Men in Groups.* New York: Random House, 1969.

West, Jessamyn. "On Friendship Between Women." *Holiday,* March, 1964.

Chapter 14

Gouldner, Alvin W. "The Norm of Reciprocity: A Preliminary Statement." *American Sociological Review,* vol. 25, no. 2, April 1960, pp. 161–78.

Lucas, Rex A. *Men in Crisis.* New York: Basic Books, 1970.

Milgram, Stanley. "The Small World Problem." *Psychology Today,* May 1967.

Chapter 15

Babchuk, N., and Bates, A. P. *Op. cit.*

Cox, Harvey. *The Secular City.* New York: The Macmillan Co., 1965.

Feagin, J. R. "A Note on the Friendship Ties of Black Urbanites." *Social Forces,* December 1970.

Gans, Herbert J. *The Levittowners. Loc. cit.*

Jones, Stella B. "Geographic Mobility As Seen by the Wife and Mother." *Journal of Marriage and the Family,* vol. 35, no. 2 (May 1973), pp. 210–17.

Liebow, E. *Tally's Corner.* Boston: Little, Brown & Co., 1967.

McAllister, R. J. "The Adaptation of Women to Residential Mobility." *Journal of Marriage and the Family,* vol. 35, no. 2 (May 1973), pp. 197–203.

McKain, J. L. "Relocation in the Military: Alienation and Family Problems." *Journal of Marriage and the Family,* vol. 35, no. 2 (May 1973), pp. 205–09.

Paine, Robert. "Anthropological Approaches to Friendship." *Humanitas,* vol. 6, no. 2, pp. 139–59.

Toffler, Alvin. *Future Shock.* New York: Random House, 1970.

Useem, R. H., *et al.* "The Function of Neighboring for the Middle-class Male." *Human Organization,* summer 1960, pp. 68–76.

Wellman, Barry. "The Multiple Communities of Modern Urbanites." Paper presented at the annual meeting of the American Institute of Planners, Boston, October 1972.

Chapter 16

Anonymous. "Friendship and Social Values in a Suburban Community." Report, summer seminar in behavioral science, University of Oregon, 1956.

Liebow, E. *Op. cit.*

Lynd, R. S., and Lynd, H. M. *Middletown.* New York: Harcourt, Brace & Co., 1929.

———. *Middletown in Transition.* New York: Harcourt, Brace & World, 1937.

Sadler, William A. "The Experience of Friendship." *Humanitas*, vol. 6, no. 2, pp. 177–209.

Zimmerman, C. C. *Successful American Families.* New York: Pageant Press, 1960.

INDEX

Index

Warner, W. Lloyd, 26, 200
Watson, G., 58, 201, 202
Weisberg, Miriam, 49, 50, 147
Wellman, Barry, 184, 203
West Indies, 37
West, Jessamyn, 202
Whitman, Walt, 43
Work, friendship role of, 99–100

Work ethic, 103, 193
Working class, 23–24, 43, 91, 105,
   127–128, 142, 146, 181, 192
Wyden, Barbara W., 201

Zande, 35
Zimmerman, C. C., 204